SERIES EDITOR: TONY HOL

## OSPREY COMBAT AIRCR

# AICHI 99 KANBAKU
# 'VAL' UNITS
# 1937–42

## OSAMU TAGAYA

OSPREY
PUBLISHING

**Front Cover**
**It is seconds prior to 0755 hrs on the morning of Sunday, 7 December 1941 at Pearl Harbor, in Hawaii, main anchorage of the US Navy's Pacific Fleet. Some 3500 m above Ford Island, in the middle of Pearl Harbor, Lt Cdr Kakuichi Takahashi of the Imperial Japanese Navy (IJN) pushes his Aichi Type 99 Carrier Bomber into its attack dive. Takahashi, the air group leader (hikotaicho) from the new IJN fleet carrier *Shokaku*, and overall leader of all dive-bombers in the first wave to assault Hawaii, is about to drop a 242 kg Type 98 Land Bomb on the seaplane ramp in front of Hangar No 6 at the southeastern end of Ford Island. All is calm down below. The sailors and airmen of the US Pacific Fleet have no inkling yet that, in less than a minute, their quiet Sunday morning will be shattered by Takahashi's bomb, the first to be dropped at Pearl Harbor. It will usher in 'the Day of Infamy', and change the course of history (*Cover artwork by Mark Postlethwaite*)**

First published in Great Britain in 2011 by Osprey Publishing
Midland House, West Way, Botley, Oxford, OX2 0PH
44-02 23rd Street, Suite 219, Long Island City, NY, 11101, USA

E-mail; info@ospreypublishing.com

Osprey Publishing is part of the Osprey Group

© 2011 Osprey Publishing Limited

A CIP catalogue record for this book is available from the British Library

ISBN: 978 1 84176 912 7
E-book ISBN: 978 1 78096 073 9

Edited by Tony Holmes
Page design by Tony Truscott
Cover Artwork by Mark Postlethwaite
Aircraft Profiles by Jim Laurier
Index by Alan Thatcher
Originated by PDQ Digital Media Solutions, Suffolk, UK
Printed in China through Bookbuilders

11 12 13 14 15   10 9 8 7 6 5 4 3 2 1

Osprey Publishing is supporting the Woodland Trust, the UK's leading woodland conservation charity by funding the dedication of trees.

**www.ospreypublishing.com**

ACKNOWLEDGEMENTS
I am deeply indebted to numerous people who gave me their enthusiastic and unstinting support in the research, writing and photo coverage for this book. Without their kind assistance, this volume would never have been written. To those veterans of the World War 2 era who actually lived through many of the events described in this book, my gratitude goes to the late Zenji Abe, the late Keiichi Arima, Kenji Hori, Hachiro Miyashita and my own father, the late Yoshio Tagaya. Among my dear friends in the military history community, my thanks go to David Aiken, William Bartsch, Michael Claringbould, Richard L Dunn, George Eleftheriou, Bruce Gamble, Lawrence J Hickey, Mark E Horan, Don Kehn Jr, James F Lansdale, James Long, John Lundstrom, Robert C Mikesh, Shigeru Nohara, Jonathan Parshall, Henry Sakaida, James Sawruk, Peter C Smith, Mark Stille, Robert Stuart, Justin Taylan, Anthony Tully, Jan Visser, Michael Wenger, Ron Werneth and Edward M Young.

# CONTENTS

CHAPTER ONE
**DIVE-BOMBING IN THE IJN 6**

CHAPTER TWO
**CHINA – FIRST BLOOD 15**

CHAPTER THREE
**PRELUDE TO PEARL HARBOR 18**

CHAPTER FOUR
**'TO-RA, TO-RA, TO-RA' 25**

CHAPTER FIVE
**SOUTHERN ADVANCE 46**

CHAPTER SIX
**ZENITH IN THE INDIAN OCEAN 55**

CHAPTER SEVEN
**CORAL SEA – THE CARRIERS CLASH 63**

CHAPTER EIGHT
**MIDWAY AND THE ALEUTIANS 76**

**APPENDICES 92**
COLOUR PLATES COMMENTARY 92
INDEX 95

# DIVE-BOMBING IN THE IJN

The British are recognised for initiating the practice of dropping a bomb from a diving aircraft in combat during World War 1, and various nations subsequently pursued the technique. However, only three – the USA, Germany and Japan – became major exponents of dive-bombing during World War 2. Perhaps it would not be too great a generalisation to say of dive-bombing that the Americans were the first to perfect it, the Germans were influenced by the American experience and the Japanese adopted it with technical help from the Germans.

The Imperial Japanese Navy (IJN) had conducted rudimentary bombing trials with diving fighters and floatplanes from the mid-1920s, noting that this method of attack achieved a significantly higher rate of hits in comparison to horizontal bombing.

Initially, dive-bombing was referred to as tokushu bakugeki, or 'special bombing', in the IJN to distinguish it from conventional horizontal bombing and to disguise the exact nature of the technique. In 1929, Yokosuka Kokutai, the air testing and evaluation centre of the IJN, undertook trials using a Type 3 Carrier Fighter (Nakajima A1N) – a licence-built British Gloster Gambet – in an effort to formally evaluate the merits of dive-bombing and to gather basic data. This was followed in 1930 by dive-bombing trials conducted by Type 3 fighters from the aircraft carriers *Kaga* and *Hosho*, when 4 kg practice bombs were used at sea against the old cruiser *Akashi*. In 1931 Type 3s from *Akagi* and *Hosho* dive-bombed the old cruiser *Chitose* with 30 kg practice bombs.

Also in 1931, the IJN ordered Nakajima Hikoki KK (Nakajima Aeroplane Co Ltd) to produce what would become Japan's first purpose-built dive-bomber based on a design by Jun-ichiro Nagahata, an aeronautical engineer with the Aircraft Division of the Naval Technical Research Institute. Nagahata had just returned from a tour of the USA, having visited a number of aircraft manufacturers including Curtiss and Vought. Nakajima design engineer Ryozo Yamamoto undertook detailed work on the project based on Nagahata's basic concept design.

The resulting machine, the Nakajima 6-Shi (for sixth year of Showa – i.e. 1931, Experimental) Carrier-based Special Bomber, was an odd-looking biplane with reverse stagger of its upper wings, and with the upper and lower wings detached from the fuselage and connected to it by struts. Exhibiting very poor longitudinal stability, the first prototype crashed in November 1932, killing the test pilot. A modified 7-Shi Carrier-based Special Bomber followed without showing much improvement, and dive-bomber development moved on to the 8-Shi.

Meanwhile, the IJN continued its dive-bombing trials. In 1932, using two Bristol Bulldog fighters that had been specially strengthened for dive-bombing, Yokosuka Kokutai successfully conducted vertical dives, ultimately using a 250 kg ordinary bomb. As the branch of the armed forces dedicated to fighting the nation's enemies at sea, the IJN referred to semi-armour-piercing bombs designed for use against warships as the tsujo bakudan (ordinary bomb). Bombs designed for use against land targets were designated as the rikujo bakudan (land bomb).

In late 1933 the IJN's first operational dive-bombing squadron embarked aboard the carrier *Ryujo*, and the development of dive-bombing techniques now commenced in an operational setting. This predated the unveiling of Germany's first operational dive-bombing unit, *Fliegergruppe Schwerin*, by almost two years.

Pending delivery of a purpose-designed dive-bomber, the *Ryujo* unit received the Nakajima Type 90 Mark 2 Model 3 Reconnaissance Seaplane (E4N3). Despite its designation, this aircraft was a wheeled-undercarriage version of the basic design, which, in turn, was a licence-built version of the Vought O2U Corsair. Although equipped for carrier operations, the Type 90 was not stressed for steep dives. This meant that diving angles in excess of 50 degrees were prohibited, and attacks had to be restricted to glide bombing descents at 35-40 degrees.

With the 8-Shi Carrier-based Special Bomber project, the IJN opened dive-bomber development to competitive bidding, inviting designs from both Nakajima and from Aichi Tokei Denki KK (Aichi Clock and Electric Co Ltd). The latter, located in Nagoya, in central Japan, had first entered the aeronautical field in 1920, and had already manufactured a number of successful floatplane designs for the IJN. During its formative years the Japanese aviation industry had sought partnerships and licensing agreements with aircraft companies in Europe and the USA in an effort to quickly absorb Western aviation technology and to catch up with them in technical and industrial capabilities. Aichi had forged close ties with the German firm of Ernst Heinkel Flugzeugwerke AG.

The IJN had previously placed an order with Heinkel for the He 50, Germany's first dive-bomber design, and it now arranged for Aichi to import a single-seat export version of this aircraft, designated the He 66, in 1934. The company's design team, headed by Tokuichiro Gomei, made modifications to the He 66, strengthening the undercarriage for carrier operations, adding a second cockpit and replacing the Siemens SAM-22B powerplant with a 580 hp Nakajima Kotobuki engine.

Aichi then submitted this modified design as its contender for the 8-Shi Carrier-based Special Bomber project, receiving the IJN's short code designation D1A1. It won the competition with ease against the Navy Arsenal/Nakajima team of Nagahata and Yamamoto, whose designs were extensive modifications of their 6-Shi and 7-Shi projects (D2Y1 and D2N1).

The D1A1 was officially adopted for service in December 1934 as the Type 94 Carrier-based Light

**Type 96 Carrier Bombers (D1A2) of 13th Ku are readied for a mission in central China in September 1937. The aeroplane at left carries a single 60 kg bomb beneath each lower wing. The Type 96 Kanbaku was the mainstay of the IJN's dive-bomber force in the China war (*via Edward M Young*)**

Bomber, Japan's first purpose-built dive-bomber to attain operational status. The letter 'D' in the IJN's short code designation system stood for the new carrier bomber category, while 'A' stood for the manufacturer, Aichi. The number 94 in the IJN's type-year designation system for operational aircraft reflected the year in which the aircraft was adopted for service – in this case the year 2594 in the Imperial Japanese calendar (1934 in the West). The term 'light' was later dropped and the designation shortened to Type 94 Carrier-based Bomber.

Unlike its stopgap predecessor (the E4N3), the Type 94 Carrier Bomber was fully capable of vertical dives. It launched Aichi on its path toward a virtual monopoly in building dive-bombers for the IJN.

Although the term kyukoka bakugeki (rapid-descent bombing) became the Japanese generic term for dive-bombing, it never appeared in the official IJN nomenclature for that mission role. Just as terms such as 'dive-bombing' or 'dive-bomber' never appeared in the official nomenclature of the US Navy (such aircraft being designated as 'scout bombers'), the IJN chose to refer to its dive-bombers simply as bakugeki-ki (bomber). IJN aircraft that could carry torpedoes but lacked dive-bombing ability were known as kogeki-ki (attack aircraft). A dive-bomber designed for carrier use was a kanjo bakugeki-ki (carrier-based bomber), often abbreviated informally to kanbaku.

The Type 94 came to feature a redesigned cockpit and streamlined covers for its main undercarriage wheels in its late production form. This was followed by an improved model, equipped with a more powerful 670 hp Nakajima Hikari engine, which retained the aerodynamic refinements of late production Type 94s. It was adopted for service as the Type 96 Carrier-based Bomber in November 1936, being given the IJN's short code designation D1A2. It became the mainstay of the IJN's dive-bomber force during the undeclared war with China starting in 1937, and was later given the Allied code name 'Susie' during the Pacific War.

From the outset, however, the IJN realised that the Type 96 was only an interim measure. The world of aviation was undergoing a technological revolution in the mid-1930s, embracing the new technology of all-metal, stressed-skin construction.

In the same month in which the Type 96 Carrier Bomber was adopted for service, Aichi began detailed design work on its successor. The 9-Shi and 10-Shi programmes of the previous two years had not included any dive-bomber projects. They had, however, included design initiatives that would lead to the Type 96 Carrier Fighter (A5M) and Type 97 Carrier Attack Aircraft (B5N and B5M) monoplanes of stressed-skin, all-metal construction – the first such designs in their respective categories to attain operational status with the IJN. With these carrier-based mission roles already well on their way to receiving revolutionary new monoplane designs, the IJN now turned its attention to re-equipping the kanbaku arm.

Koku Hombu (the IJN's Bureau of Aeronautics) issued detailed specifications for an 11-Shi Carrier-based Bomber on 11 August 1936. With the nomenclature of kanjo bakugeki-ki firmly established, the term tokushu bakugeki-ki (special bomber), which had been used hitherto for all experimental dive-bomber projects, was now discarded. The main requirements of the initial specification were as follows;

**Aichi's second prototype for the 1936 Experimental (11-Shi) Carrier-based Bomber project seen at Kagamigahara airfield in 1938. No photographs are known to exist of the first prototype, which was fitted with a 730 hp Nakajima Hikari engine as an interim measure. The second prototype, shown here, was powered by an 840 hp Mitsubishi Kinsei radial as originally intended by the project design team** (*Robert C Mikesh*)

With a 250 kg bomb load, maximum speed of 200 knots (370 km/h) or more (at an altitude of 3000 metres), endurance of five hours or more at 160 knots (296 km/h) or more (at an altitude of 3000 metres), climb to an altitude of 3000 metres in six minutes or less, landing speed of 60 knots (111 km/h) or less and a diving rate of between 3.5-5 metres per second.

Three companies, Aichi, Nakajima and Mitsubishi Jukogyo KK (Mitsubishi Heavy Industries Co Ltd), had been invited to tender design proposals. Already saddled with other major projects, Mitsubishi would drop out of the competition at the mock-up stage in the summer of 1937, leaving Aichi and Nakajima to battle it out for the contract.

At Aichi, the new project was given the company designation AM-17 (AM standing for 'Aichi Monoplane'). Tokuichiro Gomei once again headed the design team, but much of the basic work was done by his chief assistant, Toshio Ozaki. Back in April 1935, Ozaki had been part of a three-man research team despatched by Aichi to Germany for the purpose of learning new, all-metal construction techniques from the company's long-time mentor and business partner, Heinkel. The team's studies centred around the He 70 Blitz, a single-engined monoplane passenger aeroplane that had drawn considerable attention in aviation circles for its sleek, modern design and high performance. Having procured an He 70 for detailed study, the team returned home in 1936.

Aichi received word from the IJN to participate in the 11-Shi Carrier Bomber competition following Ozaki's return. During his European tour, Ozaki had witnessed a demonstration flight by the Supermarine Spitfire prototype. The smooth, elliptical wings of the fighter, like those on the He 70, convinced Ozaki that this was the shape of things to come, and was to have a strong influence on Aichi's 11-Shi Kanbaku design.

For the engine, the IJN's specifications allowed the competitors a choice of several options. Aichi's engine technology had concentrated on liquid-cooled, in line designs through the licensed manufacture of Daimler-Benz products, and senior management at Aichi was eager to have the AM-17 adopt one of the company's own engines. A powerplant based on the Daimler-Benz DB 601, then under development at Aichi, showed promise of superior performance to that of radial engines from rival companies. But it was still new and untried. Other Aichi engines already in production generated insufficient power for the project's needs. Faced with this dilemma, Ozaki sought Gomei's counsel. With the latter's support, the decision was made to adopt Mitsubishi's highly reliable Kinsei (Venus) 14-cylinder, twin-row, air-cooled radial.

With the choice of powerplant decided, the design team now focused on the airframe. Inspired by what he had witnessed in Europe, Ozaki was determined to create an all-metal, cantilevered monoplane with retractable undercarriage for the AM-17 project.

Structural strength sufficient to withstand the rigours of dive-bombing, performance greater than specified requirements and lightness of weight were the three main pillars of the design team's philosophy. Much care was taken to keep protrusions on the aircraft's surface to a minimum, and flush riveting was used throughout the airframe. The main wings were set low on the fuselage and given a double main spar. The centre section was horizontal, providing good downward visibility for the pilot and a stable platform for the undercarriage, while the outer sections were given 6 deg 30 min of dihedral. These outer wing sections, as well as both the horizontal and vertical tailplanes, were elliptical in shape, thus minimising induced drag.

A full profile view of the second prototype. The engine cowling is more elongated than that ultimately fitted to the production machine and the cockpit canopy has yet to take on its final form. Most significantly, the machine lacks the fin fillet that was added later in the development of the design (*via Shigeru Nohara*)

The airfoil chosen for the wing was the new NACA 23012 – a very thin wing for its day, which the design team thought ideal for its project, with its low minimum drag coefficient number that changed little with shifts in angle of attack. Wing thickness was 15.5 percent of chord at the root and seven percent at the tip.

The undercarriage was the one aspect of the design in which Ozaki failed to realise his dream. The cutout in the wing undersurface necessary to house a retracting undercarriage was not desirable from the standpoint of structural strength. The retraction mechanism would add weight and require a thick wing. It also became apparent to the design team that the effort needed to design the mechanism could well cause a delay in the project beyond the deadline demanded by the IJN. Furthermore, wind tunnel tests indicated that the performance requirements could be met, even with a fixed undercarriage. Thus, in the interests of simplicity, weight saving, robustness and speed of development, Aichi chose a fixed undercarriage for the AM-17.

A requirement issued on 10 May 1937 to hold the diving speed to approximately 250 knots (not to exceed 270 knots) made dive brakes a necessity. Various ideas were considered and tested in the wind tunnel. These included having part of the flap system double as dive brakes, panels which swung out from the sides of the rear fuselage near the tail, having the main undercarriage fairings split open sideways to act as brake panels and having the undercarriage itself rotate 90 degrees to provide the braking action. Ultimately, the design team settled on a pair of slats beneath the outer sections of each wing along the forward main spar, which would turn down 90 degrees to act as brakes – an arrangement virtually identical to that used on the Junkers Ju 87.

Toshio Ozaki, while freely acknowledging the great debt owed to Heinkel in the design of the AM-17, stated categorically that the design of the dive brakes was in no way a copy of those found on the Ju 87. According to Ozaki, it was an independent creation of the Aichi design team, both the Junkers and Aichi dive brakes representing examples of convergent solutions aimed at solving the same engineering problem.

Some forced changes were made during the design process. At one point the IJN lowered the maximum diving speed restriction below 250 knots, requiring an increase in the size of the dive brakes. The IJN later relented, however, reverting to a diving speed limit of 270 knots. Another change was forced on Aichi when delivery of the Kinsei powerplant was delayed. The first prototype was duly fitted with a 730 hp Nakajima Hikari (Light) Model 1 nine-cylinder radial as an interim measure.

The first flying prototype was completed on 25 December 1937 and transported from Aichi's Funakata plant in Nagoya to nearby Kagamigahara airfield, in Gifu, six days later. Following the New Year hiatus, the prototype flew for the first time on 6 January 1938.

With design work completed and the prototype built, the main initiative for development of the 11-Shi Kanbaku passed into IJN hands. Key personnel from the Naval Air Technical Arsenal responsible for the project included engineer Masao Yamana of the Aircraft Division. A rising star, he would later gain fame as the designer of the Aichi dive-bomber's successor, the sleek Suisei (Comet) Carrier Bomber (D4Y).

The IJN test pilot initially assigned to the project from the Flight Test Division was Lt Hideo Muramatsu. He was soon succeeded, however, by Lt Cdr Shoichi Suzuki, who performed most of the flight trials. The Aichi machine was given the IJN's short code designation D3A1. In close cooperation with Aichi engineers, the Air Arsenal team began to put the aircraft through its paces.

The design and construction phase of the project had progressed smoothly enough, but now, as flight testing got underway, a number of serious flaws in the aeroplane's handling characteristics appeared. Aileron control problems and a wicked tendency to snap roll during sharp turns and loops were the two main areas for concern. Resolving them required a year-and-a-half of repeated modification and testing.

The snap roll problem was traced to wingtip stall. In an effort to minimise this phenomenon, the prototype had originally been designed with wingtip washout of 1.5 degrees and two percent camber along the outer leading edge of the main wings. Using temporary balsa wood fittings, the amount of camber was progressively increased until the uncontrolled roll tendencies subsided. The degree of washout was also increased on a redesigned wing, and ultimately production aircraft would be given 2.5 degrees of washout and 2.5 percent camber near the tip.

At a later stage in the test flight programme, when elevator mass balance was increased in order to improve control response during dive pull-outs, the snap rolls reappeared. Repeated flight testing revealed that prevention of wingtip stall alone was insufficient to arrest the phenomenon, and that preservation of directional stability during high angles of attack was of central importance. The ultimate solution to the problem was the addition of a pronounced fin fillet along the top of the rear fuselage.

The aileron control problem was eventually traced to a manufacturing error on the shop floor that had inadvertently placed the centre of the aileron hinge attachment point 7 mm below the correct position shown on the original blueprints. By then much time and effort had been wasted in attempts to find a solution through the redesign of the aileron, and its attachment configuration, before the true cause of the problem was discovered.

A much-redesigned second prototype joined the test flight programme during the first half of 1938. As expected, the Hikari-powered first

**Above and top**
The two prototypes were followed by two pre-production machines in the spring of 1939. Here, the second pre-production aircraft undergoes flight testing near Nagoya. The engine cowling and the cockpit design have now taken on the appearance of the full production version. The fin fillet – the addition of which finally solved the snap roll problems that plagued the early phase of the flight test programme – is now also in evidence. The undercarriage strut fairings, however, which became thicker and more robust on full production aircraft, remain slightly thinner as on the prototypes (*Shigeru Nohara*)

prototype had proven to be badly underpowered. A Mitsubishi Kinsei Model 3, rated at 840 hp for take-off, was duly installed on the second prototype and housed in a redesigned engine cowling. The dimensions of the aircraft were also slightly increased. The wingspan on the second machine was increased to 14.5 m from 14.1 m, thus increasing wing surface area from 33 sq m to 35 sq m. The shape of the wing trailing edge had curved back inward at the root on the first prototype in classic Heinkel fashion. This was changed to a straight edge on the second aircraft, allowing the size of the flaps to be increased. Fuselage length was also slightly increased and overall weight grew by approximately 200 kg. Flight characteristics and performance improved significantly with the second aircraft.

Meanwhile, Aichi's rival, Nakajima, had finally produced its contender for the 11-Shi Kanbaku prize. The design team headed by Ryozo Yamamoto had created a slim, all-metal monoplane that was known within Nakajima as the DB and given the IJN's short code designation D3N1. Powered by an improved Hikari Model 1 Kai, nine-cylinder radial, with a maximum power rating of 820 hp, Nakajima's 11-Shi Kanbaku featured a fully retractable undercarriage that rotated through 90 degrees, allowing the wheels to retract rearward and lie flat against the wing undersurface, much like the arrangement found on the Curtiss P-36 and P-40. In the dive, the undercarriage also acted as dive brakes, being extended with the wheels parallel to the wing leading edge. When the IJN reduced its maximum diving speed specification, however, this arrangement proved inadequate.

While searching for a solution to their dive brake problem, Nakajima's designers missed the deadline for prototype submission, thereby becoming technically disqualified from the competition. They persevered, however, and found their answer in perforated flaps, similar to those used on the Douglas SBD Dauntless. With reluctant IJN acquiescence, Nakajima handed over its first prototype in March 1938. A second prototype was not delivered until the beginning of 1939.

It was now up to the Naval Air Technical Arsenal to decide which 11-Shi Kanbaku design would prevail. The two prototypes of Aichi's D3A1 were followed by two pre-production machines in March and April 1939. The last of the stability problems were ironed out on these aeroplanes during the late spring and summer of that year. More

A rare shot of the rival D3N1, Nakajima's contender in the 11-Shi competition. Although more graceful and sophisticated than Aichi's D3A1, the Nakajima machine lost out in competitive trials. The IJN was attracted to the Aichi design's greater simplicity and more robust characteristics (*Arawasi/ George Eleftheriou*)

pre-production machines and the first few production examples followed from September onward.

Even with its visibly more modern features, the performance of the D3N1 proved slightly inferior to that of the D3A1. Finally, on 16 December 1939, the IJN chose Aichi's design for operational service as the Type 99 Carrier-based Bomber. Among servicemen, the aircraft would come to be known as the 99 Kanbaku.

## TYPE 99 CARRIER-BASED BOMBER VARIANTS

### D3A1

The production model of the D3A1 was initially powered by a Kinsei Model 43 engine rated at 1000 hp for take-off. Later examples sported a slightly improved Kinsei Model 44, with take-off power rated at 1070 hp. The dimensions of the production version differed slightly again from the second prototype, with a wingspan of 14.36 m (total wing surface area of 34.9 sq m). The fuselage was slightly longer at 10.185 m.

The IJN recorded its maximum speed at 206 knots (381 km/h) and its cruising speed at 160 knots (296 km/h). The aircraft had a maximum range of 795 nautical miles (1473 km) and a service ceiling of 8070 m.

Armament consisted of two fixed, forward-firing 7.7 mm Type 97 machine guns mounted atop the engine cowling, and a single, hand-held, 7.7 mm Type 92 machine gun in the observer's cockpit. Standard bomb load was one 250 kg bomb on the centreline rack beneath the fuselage, mounted on a release arm that swung the bomb clear of the propeller arc during the dive, and one 30 kg bomb on a rack beneath the outer sections of each wing. On operations, however, bombs weighing up to 60 kg were routinely carried beneath the wings.

The outer third of the wings folded manually in compliance with IJN specifications, folding downward on the first 46 machines and folding upward from the 47th machine onward. Late production D3A1s sported propeller spinners. After the two prototypes, a total of 476 D3A1s were built, with production ending in early August 1942.

The framework of the D3A1, illustrating to good effect the robust semi-monocoque construction of the Aichi machine (*Shigeru Nohara*)

### D3A2

In June 1942 a D3A1 was fitted with a more powerful Kinsei Model 54 rated at 1300 hp for take-off and housed in a redesigned engine cowling. This became the sole prototype for an improved version of the basic design.

During 1942 the IJN adopted a new, two-digit system for aircraft

A full production D3A1, designated the Type 99 Carrier-based Bomber in IJN operational service. This is a machine of 33rd Ku, based at Surabaya, in Java, in the early summer of 1942 (*Shigeru Nohara*)

A Type 99 Carrier Bomber Model 22 (D3A2) in silhouette, giving an excellent profile view of its lines. In contrast to the original production D3A1, now retroactively designated the Model 11, the Model 22 sported a redesigned engine cowling and cockpit canopy. Additionally, the fin fillet on the Model 22 was 40 mm higher than on the Model 11. Thanks to its more powerful Mitsubishi Kinsei Model 54 engine, the Model 22 had a top speed some 25 knots faster than the Model 11, although the payload remained unchanged and range was actually reduced (*Thorpe/NARA via James F Lansdale*)

model designations. The left-hand digit indicated changes to the airframe, while the right-hand digit reflected changes in powerplant. The two digits were not sequential. Thus, for example, Model 11 would be read as 'Model One-One', not Model 11, and Model 22 would be 'Model Two-Two'. Under this system, the new Kinsei 54-powered machine became known as the Provisional Designation Type 99 Carrier-based Bomber Model 12, being given the short code designation D3A2.

Modifications were made to the airframe based on lessons learned in combat. The horizontal stabilisers were increased in size, as were the wing flaps to a slight extent. The fin fillet atop the rear fuselage was raised 40 mm and the cockpit canopy redesigned. A propeller spinner now became standard. Fuel capacity was increased with the addition of a 79-litre tank inside the front portion of the right wing for use during take-off with high-grade fuel, but engine oil capacity was reduced from 82 to 60 litres. Overall weight increased by 218 kg and, despite the increased fuel capacity, range was reduced to 730 nautical miles (1352 km). With a full payload, this dropped to 567 nautical miles (1050 km). Other aspects of the aeroplane's performance, however, improved significantly, with maximum speed jumping to 231 knots (428 km/h) and operational ceiling rising to 10,500 m. Landing speed rose to 70 knots, however.

The primary bomb load remained one 250 kg weapon, but the bomb release arm was redesigned, and the number of racks for auxiliary ordnance was increased to two per wing.

With June and July 1942 taken up with redesign work and flight testing, Aichi began production of the new D3A2 in August following re-tooling and termination of D3A1 production. Belatedly, on 7 January 1943, the Provisional Designation Model 12 was given the formal designation Type 99 Carrier-based Bomber Model 22. With the advent of the Model 22, the D3A1 was retroactively designated Type 99 Carrier-based Bomber Model 11.

Including the prototype, Aichi built 816 Model 22s until production ceased in June 1944. Separately, Showa Hikoki KK (Showa Aeroplane Co Ltd) built 201 (some sources indicate 220) examples from December 1943 until war's end. Its machines had individual engine exhaust stacks for thrust augmentation.

# CHINA – FIRST BLOOD

In November 1939, a month prior to its official acceptance as the Type 99, the first examples were sent for field evaluation to the 14th Kokutai (Ku) at Haikou, on Hainan Island in southern China. In an effort to stem the flow of supplies entering South China from Hanoi, in northern French Indochina, the Japanese launched an operation to capture Nanning, in Kwangsi Province, on 15 November. It was here that Aichi's new monoplane dive-bomber first entered combat with the 14th Ku's dive-bomber chutai under the newly arrived leadership of Lt Sadamu Takahashi. Nanning fell on 24 November, but from mid-December there followed a desperate defence against a counterattack launched by superior numbers of Chinese troops. The new dive-bombers, now officially named the Type 99 Carrier-based Bomber, provided much needed direct support to Japanese army troops.

The campaign to capture Nanning was just part of a wider effort to blockade China from the outside world. By the end of February the dive-bomber chutai of the 14th Ku had completely re-equipped with the Type 99 Kanbaku, Lt Takahashi leading 12 of the new aircraft (nine, plus three spares) into Nanning airfield from Haikou for a bombing campaign against targets in Kweichow Province. The dive-bombers flew 13 missions to the area through to June 1940, concentrating primarily on the railway junction town of Kweiyang. In addition to these sorties to the north, eight dive-bombers flew a mission against a railway bridge near Lao Cai, on the Indochinese border, on 14 May.

Meanwhile, by May 1940, the 12th Ku in central China had become the second frontline unit to operate the aircraft. The new kanbaku arrived in time to participate in the capture of Ichang, on the Yangtze River some 275 km west of Hankow (Wuhan) – site of the main Japanese airfield in central China. As in South China, the Type 99s of the 12th Ku provided direct support to ground forces. The aircraft also attacked shipping on the Yangtze River that was shuttling men and supplies between Ichang and Chiang Kai Shek's capital, Chungking, to the west. Keiichi Arima, then a young lieutenant with the 12th Ku, recalled the thrill of dive-bombing river traffic in the Yangtze Gorges, which soared up west of Ichang;

'With sheer cliffs of over 1000 m on either side, we threaded our way down to the river below, being careful not to hit the cliff face as we dove. After releasing our bomb on the target, we had to twist the aeroplane as we climbed back up, making sure, once again, not to collide with the mountain walls around us. It was dangerous, yet thrilling sport.'

Ichang fell to the Japanese on 12 June. Control of the small airstrip there made it possible for single-engined aircraft to attack Chungking. Starting on 3 September, the Type 99s flew a series of missions against

Two early-production D3A1s fly in close formation for the benefit of the camera (*Author*)

Chungking, staging through Ichang each time. On the 12th, nine of them, led by Lt Miyuki Terashima, targeted warehouses. Next day, eight hit the city's cement factory, while the escort of A6M Zero-Sen fighters made the date famous as it gave the latter aircraft their combat debut.

12th Ku dive-bombers next appeared over Chungking on 15 and 16 September, and again on 13 October. But on 25 October one was lost when its oil line was hit by ground fire and it crashed east of Chungking – the only Type 99 lost in combat over China. Pilot Flyer 1st Class (F 1/c) Harada, was captured and observer F 1/c Satoshi Kuramochi killed.

With ground operations in central China stalled following the capture of Ichang, the 12th Ku disbanded its kanbaku chutai in November.

Meanwhile, the fall of France to Nazi Germany in June 1940 had presented a major strategic opportunity for Japan. The French, who had previously resisted Japanese pressure to stop the shipment of supplies to China along the Hanoi-Kunming railway, now relented. Agreement was reached in September, allowing Japanese forces to occupy northern French Indochina. Nine Type 99s of the 14th Ku, along with the unit's Zero-sens, deployed to Gia Lam airfield, near Hanoi, on 7 October 1940. With the Japanese in Hanoi, the Indochinese supply route to China was closed for good. But supplies still flowed in along the Burma Road further west. Burma was not within Japan's grasp – at least, not yet.

Flying out of Hanoi from October, the dive-bombers and fighters of the 14th Ku flew numerous missions against Kunming and other targets in Yunnan Province along the Chinese end of the Burma Road.

## JOINING THE FLEET

In 1940 the IJN possessed a total of six aircraft carriers. Four of them were major fleet carriers, namely the 41,300-ton converted battlecruiser *Akagi*, the 42,541-ton converted battleship *Kaga*, the smaller, but more modern and purpose-built 18,800-ton *Soryu* and its near-sister, the 20,250-ton *Hiryu*. These ships all operated fighters, bombers (i.e. dive-bombers) and attack aircraft (i.e. torpedo bombers), the three main categories of carrier-based machines. The small 12,732-ton *Ryujo*, first to embark a kanbaku chutai in 1933, was in reserve status for most of 1940, while the old 10,797-ton *Hosho*, Japan's first aircraft carrier, normally did not carry dive-bombers.

*Hiryu* is seen here on sea trials in 1939. The vessel, and its sister ship *Soryu*, formed 2nd Koku Sentai of Kido Butai and were very active during the first part of the war. Neither ship was present at the Battle of the Coral Sea, but both were committed to the Midway operation, where they were sunk by American carrier-based aircraft (*US Naval Historical Center*)

The Type 99 Carrier-based Bomber was displayed to the public for the first time when it participated in the fly past conducted as part of the special naval review of 11 October 1940. This event, celebrating the 2600th year of the nation's founding according to the imperial Japanese calendar, took place off Yokohama shortly before the new dive-bomber began to re-equip carrier-based units. The aircraft shown are from Yokosuka Kokutai, the elite service test unit of the IJN based adjacent to the great naval base of Yokosuka. The latter was in turn only a short distance down the coast from the major commercial port of Yokohama. Immediately ahead of the Type 99 are Mitsubishi Type 96 Attack Aeroplanes (G3Ms) (*IJN*)

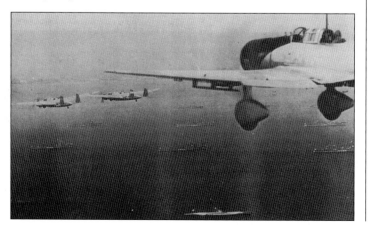

During the 1930s, the big 'battlewagon' conversions *Akagi* and *Kaga* were usually assigned to 1st Koku Sentai (Carrier Division) and operated with First Fleet, the IJN's main battle line. When *Soryu* and *Hiryu* joined the fleet in 1937 and 1939, respectively, they were assigned to 2nd Koku Sentai, which operated with Second Fleet, the cruiser scouting force.

For much of 1940, dive-bomber squadrons of the fleet still operated biplane Type 96 Carrier Bombers. Conversion to the Type 99 began in November of that year, and it was mainly completed by January 1941.

Assignment of carrier divisions to the battleship and cruiser fleets reflected standard naval doctrine in the interwar years, which continued to cast aviation in a supporting role to the 'big guns' of the fleet. But the tremendous strides made in aircraft technology during the 1930s had not gone unnoticed. As the decade drew to a close, consensus began to grow that the aeroplane was becoming a powerful weapon in its own right. The evolution of the IJN's annual fleet exercises sheds interesting light on this trend. The training programme for Fiscal Year 1939 (for training purposes, the IJN used a fiscal year that began on 1 December of the previous calendar year and ended on 30 November of the year in question) was based on a classic fleet engagement scenario. However, for the first time it emphasized the coordinated use of air attack by fighters, dive-bombers and carrier- and land-based attack aircraft.

During the course of the 1939 training programme, on 30 August, the reigns of Combined Fleet command passed to Vice-Adm Isoroku Yamamoto (promoted to full admiral on 15 November 1940), one of the most air-minded of Japan's naval leaders. Under his direction, the training programme for Fiscal Year 1940 placed carrier aviation under a centralised command for the first time.

Even more significantly, the exercises were no longer conducted within the framework of a fleet engagement, but on the premise that air attack would be the prime instrument of action against an enemy fleet. Simulated air strikes conducted against warships during March 1940 proved particularly impressive, leading Rear Adm Jisaburo Ozawa, who had held the centralised command during the exercises, to formally recommend that a centralised fleet command for air units be made permanent. Similar recommendations had been forthcoming from the IJN's Research Committee on Aviation Procedures the previous June, and there were those within the Naval General Staff who concurred.

Such convergence of opinion resulted in the formation of First Air Fleet on 10 April 1941. This organisation formally brought together almost all of the carriers of the Combined Fleet for the first time. At its formation, First Air Fleet controlled 1st Koku Sentai (*Akagi* and *Kaga*), 2nd Koku Sentai (*Soryu* and *Hiryu*) and 4th Koku Sentai (*Ryujo*). 3rd Koku Sentai, centred on *Hosho* and the new light carrier *Zuiho*, remained with the battleships of First Fleet. Such a concentration of carrier-based air power under a single command was unprecedented in naval history.

A line-up of factory fresh Type 99s newly assigned to the carrier *Akagi*. This photograph was taken in April 1941, shortly after the formation of 1st Air Fleet, of which *Akagi* became the flagship. The aircraft nearest to the camera is 'AI-205'. Note that these dive-bombers do not yet display the colour-coded band on the rear fuselage that indicated their specific carrier assignment. This would soon become a standard marking feature of aeroplanes assigned to 1st Air Fleet (*Shigeru Nohara*)

# PRELUDE TO PEARL HARBOR

Ever since Adm Heihachiro Togo's stunning victory over the Russian Imperial Fleet in 1905, orthodox thinking in the IJN had called for a decisive fleet engagement as the key to victory in any naval conflict. Following its triumph in the Russo-Japanese War of 1904–05, the IJN came to see the US Navy as its main potential adversary. Year after year, both in tabletop manoeuvres and in fleet exercises, the war planners of the IJN focused on a single theme – a showdown with the American fleet as the latter steamed westward across the Pacific. Isoroku Yamamoto disagreed with such thinking.

None of the war games or fleet manoeuvres had demonstrated decisive victory for the Japanese side, while the rise of air power made it questionable whether a major engagement between battle fleets would even occur at all. More than most Japanese of his generation, Yamamoto understood the vast superiority of American manpower and industrial might. He was certain that any war with the United States based on conventional strategy would lead to Japan's ultimate defeat, and was personally against war with America. Yet, as Commander-in-Chief Combined Fleet, he felt it his duty to devise a strategy that would give Japan a fighting chance in such an unequal contest. The only solution, he reasoned, was to inflict a massive blow on the US Navy at the very start of hostilities in order to even the odds, and then to maintain the initiative, denying the Americans a chance to bring their superior strength to bear in a war of attrition.

Yamamoto began to consider the idea of an air attack on Pearl Harbor seriously at the end of November 1940, having been deeply impressed by the nocturnal British air raid on the Italian fleet at Taranto earlier that month. By then the training programme for Fiscal Year 1941 had already been established and was about to be implemented. The IJN's conduct during the course of 1941 would be a study in metamorphosis of what began as contingency planning and ended in deliberate preparation to wage war.

During the course of the 1941 training programme, starting on 1 February, 2nd Koku Sentai took part in Operation *S* – a show of force around French Indochina and the Gulf of Siam, as Japan mediated a ceasefire of a border conflict between the French and the Thais. On 2 March, following the peaceful conclusion of Operation *S*, the flight echelons of *Soryu* and *Hiryu* took part in bombing the Fujian coast in central China, marking the first time that carrier-based Type 99 Kanbaku had dropped bombs on hostile territory.

Vice-Adm Chuichi Nagumo (a torpedo expert with no experience in aviation) was chosen to command First Air Fleet upon its formation in

April 1941. Given the command for reasons of seniority, he was wise enough to surround himself with officers that had aviation backgrounds. His chief of staff, Rear Adm Ryunosuke Kusaka, came to his new post following command of the land-based 24th Koku Sentai (Air Flotilla), while his senior air staff officer, Cdr Minoru Genda, a former fighter pilot, moved up from 1st Koku Sentai staff.

On 10 April – the day that Nagumo assumed command – orders were issued in his name outlining the training programme for First Air Fleet. Listed as top priority was a surprise attack on airfields using the full strength of the air fleet *en masse*.

On the Asian mainland the dive-bombers of the 14th Ku continued to raid Yunnan from their base at Hanoi during 1941, interdicting the Chinese portion of the Burma Road and its continuation northeast past Kunming. In early June they focused on 'bridge-busting', destroying the vital suspension bridge over the Beipan Jiang between Kunming and Kweiyang on the 8th.

Japan's entry into northern French Indochina the previous autumn had ostensibly been for the purpose of bringing the war in China to a close through the blockade of its southern supply routes. But Japan had also adopted a national policy of expanding its influence southward at every opportunity. In June 1941, in order to head off growing American and British influence over the French, the Japanese decided to occupy southern French Indochina as well.

For the second time in just a matter of months, 2nd Koku Sentai was alerted for deployment to Indochina on 5 July. The forces involved in Operation *Fu-go*, as the move into southern French Indochina was known, departed Hainan Island for their objective on the 25th. With the Vichy French government in Indochina having bowed to Japanese diplomatic pressure, the advance was peaceful. The convoy of 39 army transports under warship escort, with air patrols provided by seaplanes and aircraft from *Soryu* and *Hiryu*, made for an intimidating sight. Along with other aircraft types, the 14th Ku sent 12 Type 99 Carrier Bombers to Saigon on 31 July.

The Americans, British and Dutch were thoroughly alarmed by Japan's move into southern French Indochina, which they saw as a direct threat to their own colonies in the region. Political and economic repercussions were swift. On all sides, feelings grew that the outbreak of war in the Far East beyond China was now inevitable.

## THE HAWAIIAN OPERATION

Naval General Staff stood at the pinnacle of the IJN's command structure, and had the task of devising Japan's naval strategy. Combined Fleet, as the highest command afloat, was tasked with carrying out the Naval General Staff's plans. However, Adm Yamamoto's stature within the IJN, and his own strong views on strategy, would strain this relationship between the two commands.

Naval General Staff began to plan in earnest for a simultaneous war against the USA, Britain and the Netherlands East Indies in June 1941. Despite strong requests from members of Combined Fleet staff to include an attack on Pearl Harbor in such plans, Naval General Staff deemed the operation too risky and declined to do so. Heated debate between the two staffs followed in August, but when an initial version of Naval General Staff's multi-national war plan was completed later that month, it still failed to incorporate an attack on Pearl Harbor. Meanwhile, with Yamamoto's approval, Combined Fleet staff took the unusual step of developing their own Pearl Harbor attack plans that summer, fully aware that such thinking did not figure in Naval General Staff's grand strategy.

The matter remained unresolved when key officers from Naval General Staff, Combined Fleet, First Air Fleet and Eleventh Air Fleet met on 19–20 August to discuss the needs of naval aviation in coming months. One of the key decisions made during this two-day conference was the reinforcement of First Air Fleet with an additional koku sentai. It was also decided that a single officer should command all carrier flight echelons within First Air Fleet. He was to also be given the responsibility of training all naval aviators under a unified command structure. Lt Cdr Mitsuo Fuchida was chosen for this demanding role, and he duly reported aboard the carrier *Akagi* on 25 August as its senior flying group leader (hikotaicho).

Until reorganised into independent air units in 1944, the aircraft and aircrew aboard IJN aircraft carriers were considered part of the ship's complement. Thus, traditionally, the captain of each individual carrier had been in charge of training his ship's airmen. This changed with Fuchida's arrival. While the carriers returned to their home ports between late August and early October 1941 for refit, their flight echelons continued their training at airfields in Kyushu, now all coordinated under Fuchida's command. The dive-bombers of 1st Koku Sentai went to Tomioka, midway up the east coast of Kyushu, while those of 2nd Koku Sentai were based at Kasanohara, near the south coast.

The IJN went to full mobilisation on 1 September. The same day saw the formation of 5th Koku Sentai, centred around the newly commissioned 29,800-ton fleet carrier *Shokaku*. A sister ship, *Zuikaku*, joined it on 25 September. Simultaneously with its formation, 5th Koku Sentai was incorporated into First Air Fleet.

In preparation for war with the West, the IJN withdrew almost all of its forces from China. The 12th and 14th Ku, the last sizeable naval air units on the continent, were both disbanded on 15 September, bringing to a close dive-bomber operations against southern China. Many airmen from both kokutai were transferred to 5th Koku Sentai.

Under the strictest secrecy, Combined Fleet held war games for the Hawaiian operation at the Naval War College in Tokyo on 16–17 September. Here, the 'Blue force' (Japanese) was discovered by a 'Red force' (American) patrol aeroplane on the evening before the

**Shokaku** in August 1941, just after completion. It was the lead ship in the most successful class of wartime Japanese carriers. After being damaged during the Battle of the Coral Sea, the vessel went on to see action in the carrier battles of the Eastern Solomons and Santa Cruz, before finally being sunk by a submarine in June 1944 during the Battle of the Philippine Sea (*US Naval Historical Center*)

planned air strike. In two days of battle, 'Blue' sank four of 'Red's' battleships, two carriers and three cruisers, damaged several other ships and destroyed 180 of 'Red's' aircraft. But 'Red's' counterstrike sank three of 'Blue's' carriers, left a fourth seriously damaged and destroyed 127 'Blue' aircraft, including 36 dive-bombers. The judges were persuaded to lessen 'Blue's' carrier losses, but it was clear to all concerned that if the operation was to have any chance of success, surprise would be essential.

Lt Cdr Fuchida (soon to be promoted to full commander on 15 October) had to ensure smooth coordination among all the squadrons of First Air Fleet's carriers, but training was also coordinated within each mission role. Thus, the dive-bombers of 1st and 2nd Koku Sentai trained together under the direction of *Soryu* Hikotaicho, Lt Cdr Takashige Egusa, who was recognised throughout the fleet as the most accomplished leader of the kanbaku corps.

Dive-bombing was defined in the IJN as anything steeper than 45 degrees, and was generally performed at angles between 55 and 65 degrees in the final dive – somewhat shallower than the 70-degree dives of their US Navy counterparts. Standard altitude for bomb release had been 800 metres, but, in an unrelenting effort to improve bombing accuracy, Egusa lowered the limit to 600 metres, then to 400 – the absolute minimum for a safe dive in a Type 99.

As the pilot concentrated on the target, the observer in the rear seat focused all his attention on the altimeter and read off the descent in altitude. Each revolution of the indicator needle represented 500 metres. Miscounting the number of revolutions would prove fatal. At the instant the observer read out 400 metres the pilot would release his bomb and yank back on his control column with every ounce of his strength. Shinsaku Yamakawa, a young enlisted kanbaku pilot from *Kaga* recalled the gruelling nature of the training. 'At the moment of pull out, huge pressure, amounting to 6-6.5 Gs, would crush us down. Our heads would get squashed between our shoulders and red stars seemed to shoot out from our eyeballs before we blacked out.'

'AII-252', a Type 99 from the carrier *Kaga*, flies past Mount Fuji during a training exercise in the early autumn of 1941. Note that the aircraft's overall silver finish has been replaced by a shade of light olive grey and, although most of the tail section is missing from this photograph, its red colouring has now been discontinued (*Shigeru Nohara*)

When the crew regained consciousness, their aeroplane would typically be flying a mere 20 metres above the ground.

While the aircrews trained around the clock, debate at the highest levels continued to cast a cloud on the Hawaiian operation. By late September, Naval General Staff had finally become receptive to Yamamoto's plan, but the Combined Fleet commander-in-chief also faced dissent among his own ranks. The leaders of both First Air Fleet and Eleventh Air Fleet were opposed. They wanted the fleet carriers assigned to the conquest of Southeast Asia – the main war objective. 'What if the US fleet mounts an air strike on the homeland during the course of our southern operations?' Yamamoto asked. 'So long as I am Commander-in-Chief Combined Fleet, I am determined to carry out a surprise attack on Hawaii'. With that, everyone fell into line.

Finalisation of plans for the Pearl Harbor strike was ordered on 5 October. Two days later the operation was revealed for the first time to all key air officers within First Air Fleet down to hikotaicho level. During the following week, the word also went out to the buntaicho (squadron leaders).

Debate still lingered over how many fleet carriers to assign to the Hawaiian operation, there still being talk of using some of the big carriers to support the southern advance. It was not until 19 October that Adm Osami Nagano, Chief of the Naval General Staff, with a reporting line directly to the imperial throne, finally gave his assent to Yamamoto's plan of using all six fleet carriers against Hawaii. Formal orders for the Hawaiian operation were issued by Naval General Staff to Combined Fleet the very next day.

The tactical organisation for the operation, built around the big carriers of First Air Fleet, would soon become known as Kido Butai (Mobile Force), commanded by Vice Adm Nagumo. Its vessels assembled for the first time on 2 November, and a full dress rehearsal of the operation took place from 4 to 6 November, with the carriers launching two-wave strikes against the main body of the Combined Fleet at anchor in Saeki Bay in Kyushu.

Absent from the November dress rehearsal were the airmen of 5th Koku Sentai, who had only just come together during September. Indeed, in the case of *Zuikaku*, the last aircrew did not report in until October. While many were experienced flyers individually, they had not

Type 99 'AI-208' was an early aircraft assigned to *Akagi's* 2nd dive-bomber chutai. The letter 'A' is the machine's tail code, indicating its assignment to 1st Koku Sentai, while the Roman numeral 'I' denoted the carrier *Akagi* – the first vessel within the koku sentai according to the administrative order of battle (which was not necessarily the same as making the vessel a flagship). A system of colour-coded stripes on the rear fuselage would become a standard part of the unit marking system within 1st Air Fleet, with *Akagi's* aeroplanes coming to sport a single red stripe during the summer of 1941 (*Author*)

trained together sufficiently as a group. Moreover, most of them came from land-based units, and were simply not up to the standards of carrier proficiency displayed by their comrades in 1st and 2nd Koku Sentai. Flightdeck accidents were numerous as the airmen of *Zuikaku* and *Shokaku* concentrated on the basics of carrier operations during the short training period granted to them,

By 19 November all flight echelons were back aboard their respective carriers. With much speculation among the rank and file as to their destination, the vessels of Kido Butai individually made their way north to barren Hitokappu Bay, in the Kurile Islands – jumping-off point for the Hawaiian operation. The carriers had all arrived there by 23 November, and the next day flight crews from all six vessels were assembled aboard Adm Nagumo's flagship *Akagi* as the air leaders of Kido Butai made final plans for the attack. Now, at last, all non-commissioned airmen ranks received word of the Pearl Harbor mission.

An attack in two waves made practical sense, as the capacity of each carrier's flightdeck could not accommodate the ship's entire aircraft complement in a single launch. The first wave would include all the dive-bombers from 5th Koku Sentai, whose perceived lower level of skill consigned them to attacking the airfields at Ford Island, Hickam and Wheeler. The second wave would include all dive-bombers from 1st and 2nd Koku Sentai, assigned to attack ships in harbour. IJN doctrine held that the 250 kg payload of the dive-bombers was ineffective against battleship armour. Target priorities for the kanbaku, therefore, were aircraft carriers first, then cruisers and, lastly, battleships or other warships of opportunity.

Following months of training, the airmen of Kido Butai were at their peak. Mute testimony to the excruciating regimen they had endured were the 32 deaths from among their ranks during the 1941 training season. Fourteen of them were kanbaku men. Morale was truly high, nevertheless.

During the briefing on 24 November, 1st Air Fleet communications staff officer Lt Cdr Kanjiro Ono explained to the assembled airmen that, in the event of a forced landing, the aircraft in trouble would be allowed to radio its position as an exception to the rule of strict radio silence prior to the actual attack. At this, Lt Takehiko Chihaya, leader of *Akagi's* dive-bombers, objected. 'With this crucial battle before us in which the fate of Japan is at stake, I am against transmitting any radio signals for whatever reason before the attack'. Turning to his comrades, Chihaya said, 'If our engines fail, let us go silently to our deaths'. In the self-sacrificial spirit of the bushido warrior code, all agreed.

*Zuikaku* in 1941. At this point the vessel was virtually identical to its sister ship *Shokaku*. With the exception of Midway, *Zuikaku* participated in every carrier battle of the war (*Yamato Museum*)

Kido Butai weighed anchor for its fateful mission on the grey, overcast morning of 26 November. The constant rolling and pitching of the flightdecks from the notoriously rough winter weather in the north Pacific made every anti-submarine patrol take-off and landing a supreme challenge. For the first few days on board *Hiryu*, aeroplanes returning from patrol would shed their bombs into the sea before landing, in keeping with standard safety procedures. Thereafter, however, aircrew were ordered to bring their bombs back – a graphic illustration of the logistical shoestring on which Japan was about to launch the Pacific War.

Landing on the heaving, rain-soaked flightdeck with bombs still attached left absolutely no margin for error. On one occasion, dive-bomber observer Flight Petty Officer 3rd Class (FPO 3/c) Tatsuo Itazu recalled seeing the impact of an aeroplane's landing dislodge one of its 60 kg bombs, which then went scooting down the flightdeck. The bomb failed to explode, but it gave everyone on *Hiryu's* flightdeck a good scare.

On board *Zuikaku*, dive-bomber leader Lt Akira Sakamoto came by the hangar deck and asked his crew chief for a paintbrush and some white enamel paint. He knew he would be leading the attack on Wheeler Field, situated in the middle of Oahu. With the attacking force flying down from the north, he would be dropping the first bomb of the entire operation, several minutes before Lt Cdr Kakuichi Takahashi of *Shokaku* would drop the first bomb on Ford Island, in the middle of Pearl Harbor itself. With paintbrush in hand, Sakamoto wrote 'Kaisen hekito dai-ichi dan' ('Very first bomb of the opening of the war') on the 242 kg Type 98 Land Bomb he would be delivering to the Americans.

On 1 December Kido Butai crossed the International Dateline (180 degrees longitude) and entered the Western Hemisphere. Next day, the task force received the fateful message 'Niitaka yama nobore 1208' ('Climb Mt Niitaka 1208'), signifying the opening of hostilities at 0 hour on 8 December (still 7 December east of the International Dateline). Until then, the possibility had remained that the task force might be ordered to abort its mission and head home. However, with diplomatic negotiations in Washington, D.C. at an impasse, Japan's top leaders had finally decided on war. Kido Butai, and the nation, was now committed to hostile action.

As the task force steamed closer to Hawaii, a steady stream of information flowed from Naval General Staff in Tokyo, relaying detailed reports on ship movements at Pearl Harbor sent by Takeo Yoshikawa, the IJN's intelligence agent at the Japanese Consulate in Honolulu. His communiques were of great help to the airmen of Kido Butai, including his cousin, WO Keijiro Yoshikawa, a young dive-bomber shotaicho (section leader) on board *Hiryu*. But Takeo Yoshikawa's final report, received on 7 December (Tokyo Time), detailing events of the 5th, frustrated the kanbaku men no end. The carrier USS *Lexington* (CV-2) had departed Pearl Harbor that day. The men already knew from a previous report that USS *Enterprise* (CV-6) had left Pearl on 28 November.

It was now clear that the American aircraft carriers – priority targets for the dive-bombers – would be absent when they struck the next day. Most of the heavy cruisers were also out. But the battleships were in port, looking forward to a peaceful Sunday morning.

# 'TO-RA, TO-RA, TO-RA'

Activity aboard the six carriers of Kido Butai was anything but peaceful. By 0130 hrs local Hawaii Time on Sunday, 7 December (2100 hrs 7 December Tokyo Time), the flightdeck crews had begun spotting the aircraft of the first wave strike. By 0330 hrs the night reverberated with the sound of engines being revved up by maintenance men as bugles were blown to rouse the aircrew from their slumber. After breakfast, and having changed into their flight gear, many airmen paid their respects at their ship's Shinto shrine (one was carried aboard every warship in the IJN), then made their way topside.

Following final briefings on the flightdeck, the flyers dispersed to their assigned aircraft at 0530 hrs, climbed aboard and, one by one, began to start their engines for the actual take-off. At 0600 hrs on 7 December 1941 (0130 hrs on 8 December in Japan), 230 miles north of Oahu, the aircraft of Nagumo's first attack wave began to take off.

Having scoured the length and breadth of the IJN air service in search of aeroplanes to boost the size of their air groups, the six carriers boasted a total strength of 399 aircraft. Flagship *Akagi* carried 21 Type 0 Mark 1 Carrier-based Fighters (A6M2) (two chutai of nine aeroplanes each, plus three spares), 18 Type 99 Carrier-based Bombers (D3A1) (two chutai) and 27 Type 97 Mark 3 Carrier-based Attack Aircraft (B5N2) (three chutai). Sistership *Kaga* carried 21 Zero-Sens, 27 Type 99s and 27 Type 97s. The smaller *Soryu* and *Hiryu* of 2nd Koku Sentai each embarked 21 Zero-sens and 18 each of the other two aircraft types. *Zuikaku* and *Shokaku* of 5th Koku Sentai each carried 18 Zero-sens, 27 Type 99s (*Zuikaku* may have only had 26, as according to dive-bomber mechanic MPO 1/c Shuichi Sugino a kanbaku ditched at the time of departure from Japan and was not replaced) and 27 Type 97s.

The first wave consisted of 183 of these aeroplanes, 89 of them Type 97 Attack Aircraft from 1st and 2nd Koku Sentai. Forty-nine were configured as horizontal bombers, armed with armour-piercing 800 kg bombs, while the remaining 40 carried torpedoes. All were headed for the US Pacific Fleet at anchor in Pearl Harbor, and especially for 'Battleship Row', the capital ships being moored along the southeast side of Ford Island in the middle of the harbour.

All six carriers contributed Zero-Sens to the total of 43 escort fighters, while the dive-bombers of the first wave all came from 5th Koku Sentai. *Shokaku* launched 26 of its 27 Type 99s, one aeroplane being grounded due to mechanical problems. *Zuikaku* also launched 26, but one returned with engine trouble. Thus, in the end, *Zuikaku* contributed 25 kanbaku to the first wave, for a total of 51 Type 99s. All dive-bombers were armed with a single 242 kg Type 98 Land Bomb for use against Oahu's airfields.

Despite pitching flightdecks, the superbly trained pilots of this aerial armada took just 15 minutes to complete their take-off runs and join up in formation. Only one aeroplane, a fighter from *Soryu*, ditched on take-off, its pilot being picked up by the carrier's chase destroyer. Led by Cdr Mitsuo Fuchida, flying in the observer's seat of *Akagi's* lead Type 97 horizontal bomber, the huge formation flew one large circuit over the task force and then headed south. Fuchida's horizontal bombers flew at an altitude of 3000 m, while 200 m below and 500 m behind them to starboard flew the torpedo-bombers. The dive-bombers, led by Shokaku Hikotaicho Lt Cdr Kakuichi Takahashi, with Lt(jg) Seizo Koizumi in the rear seat, flew 500 m above and 1000 m behind to port, while the fighters maintained top cover some 300 m above them all.

Cdr Fuchida managed to home in on Honolulu radio station KGMB, which had been broadcasting all-night music for the benefit of B-17s expected in from California, and guided his formation toward the mellow tones of Hawaiian music. The station even obliged him with a weather report – 'Partly sunny, with cloud cover over the mountains with a base of 3500 ft. Good visibility, with winds out of the north at ten knots'.

With clouds that low, Fuchida judged that the planned approach from the northeast over the Koolau Mountains along the windward side of the island would be too dangerous. Deciding to fly down the western (leeward) side and approach Pearl Harbor from the south, Fuchida turned to starboard as he spotted Kahuku Point at the northern tip of Oahu through his binoculars at 0738 hrs.

Meanwhile, the carriers of Kido Butai had turned back into the wind a few minutes past 0700 hrs and launched the aeroplanes of the second wave from 0715 hrs. A total of 170 aircraft had taken off in this second strike group, led by *Zuikaku* Hikotaicho, Lt Cdr Shigekazu Shimazaki, personally flying the vessel's lead Type 97 Attack Aircraft. All 54 Type 97s of the second wave (27 each from *Zuikaku* and *Shokaku*) were armed as high-level bombers, with a mixture of 250 kg and 60 kg bombs. Once again, 5th Koku Sentai airmen were assigned to hit airfield targets.

The fighter escort for the second strike came from just the four carriers of 1st and 2nd Koku Sentai.

The centrepiece of the second strike was the force of Type 99 Carrier Bombers from 1st and 2nd Koku Sentai, each aeroplane being armed with one 250 kg Type 99 Ordinary Bomb for use against warships at Pearl Harbor. This force was led by *Soryu* Hikotaicho, Lt Cdr Takashige Egusa, with WO Miki Ishii as his observer/navigator. *Soryu*, *Hiryu* and *Akagi* each contributed 18 kanbaku, while *Kaga* sortied 26, with one

The pilot of a Type 99 carrying a single 250 kg ordinary bomb under its centreline opens the throttle of his aircraft as it gains speed for take-off from *Kaga* at 0715 hrs, thus marking the start of the second wave strike (*Michael Wenger*)

aeroplane grounded due to engine trouble. However, of the 80 Type 99s that had taken-off, one each from *Soryu* and *Hiryu* aborted with poorly running engines, leaving 78 bound for Pearl Harbor. The dropout from *Hiryu* was its kanbaku leader, Lt Michio Kobayashi. He was livid upon returning to his carrier, stamping his feet on the flightdeck in frustration. One of *Hiryu's* fighters also aborted, leaving 35 in the escort, for a total of 167 in the second wave strike.

Seeing no change in the early Sunday calm, with no American aeroplanes or anti-aircraft fire visible, Cdr Fuchida felt that surprise had been achieved. At 0740 hrs, just northeast of Kahuku Point, he reached out from his cockpit and fired a single flare – the signal to deploy for attack under 'surprise achieved' conditions. The torpedo-bombers surged forward and started to swing out to starboard as they shed altitude, but the fighters above failed to respond. After an interlude of about ten seconds, Fuchida fired his flare pistol again. The fighters saw it this time, but so did Lt Cdr Takahashi, the dive-bomber leader, who mistook the second flare for the double 'surprise lost' signal. Much to Fuchida's annoyance, Takahashi charged forward and climbed for altitude, convinced he was now supposed to strike first. The carefully planned attack sequence had gone awry, but it mattered little. The Americans below still had no inkling of what was about to hit them.

At 0745 hrs Fuchida followed his flare signal with a radio transmission to all aeroplanes of the first wave to deploy for attack readiness. The Type 99s, which had swung wide to starboard as the entire formation spread out, crossed back over to port above the flightpath of the Type 97s and split up as they reached 4000 m. Lt Akira Sakamoto swung *Zuikaku's* 25 kanbaku eastward to attack Wheeler Field – the USAAC's main fighter base on Oahu, near the middle of the island – while Takahashi hurried southeast toward Pearl Harbor with *Shokaku's* 26 Type 99s.

At 0749 hrs Fuchida's radioman, FPO 1/c Norinobu Mizuki, repeatedly transmitted • • — • • ('To, To, To, To'), which was the coded signal for 'Zengun totsugeki seyo' ('All forces charge!').

*Zuikaku's* Type 99s, which were virtually overhead Wheeler already, responded instantly. Sakamoto and his two subordinate buntaicho, Lts Tamotsu Ema and Chikahiro Hayashi, led their respective chutai in from different directions and wreaked havoc among the American aeroplanes on the ground. In a misguided effort not to alarm the civilian population by dispersing the aircraft, and to make them easier to guard against imagined saboteurs, the aeroplanes had been parked wingtip to wingtip in neat rows in front of the hangars. They made easy targets.

Following the bombing, the kanbaku went down to strafe the parked aeroplanes and hangars, as well as buildings at adjacent Schofield Barracks. The strafers went in extremely low. In Sakamoto's chutai, WO Susumu Koyama's Type 99 (piloted by FPO 1/c Toshio Inagaki – IJN multi-seat aircraft were commanded by the senior-ranking crewmember aboard, who was often the observer rather than the pilot) returned to *Zuikaku* trailing some 20 metres of telephone cable wrapped around its dive brake and tail wheel. This had been ripped off telephone poles during a strafing run.

A Type 99 from the second wave accelerates past *Kaga's* island, cheered on by the ship's crew (*Michael Wenger*)

*Zuikaku's* dive-bomber leader, Lt Akira Sakamoto, led the attack on Wheeler Field, situated in the middle of Oahu. He would drop the first bomb of the entire operation, and also lead the carrier's Type 99s in the attack on Colombo on 5 April 1942 and the sinking of HMS *Hermes* four days later (*Author*)

A well-known shot of Wheeler Field under attack by the first wave of IJN aircraft. Wheeler was the assigned target for dive-bombers from *Zuikaku*, and was the first target bombed on 7 December 1941. The USAAC fighters on the airfield were parked wingtip-to-wingtip in a misguided effort to make them easier to guard against imagined saboteurs. This in turn made them easy targets for the dive-bombers (*NA 80-G-30555 via Mike Wenger*)

In just 15 minutes the attackers had struck over half of the 153 aircraft at Wheeler. The base was later strafed by dive-bombers and fighters from the second wave, but it was the first wave attack, primarily the dive-bombing, that destroyed or damaged most of the 83 P-40B/Cs and P-36As lost on the field. *Zuikaku's* Type 99s all returned without loss.

A minute or two after *Zuikaku's* Type 99s had commenced their attack on Wheeler, Cdr Fuchida still saw no sign of activity at Pearl Harbor up ahead. Convinced that surprise had indeed been achieved, at 0752 hrs he ordered Mizuki to rap out • • — • • • • ('To-Ra, To-Ra, To-Ra') three times, this being the signal for 'surprise achieved'. This signal has often been misinterpreted as 'Tora, Tora, Tora' (i.e. 'Tiger, Tiger, Tiger'), but according to Lt Cdr Kanjiro Ono, the fleet communications staff officer who chose this code signal, it was simply selected as a clear phonetic combination.

Having approached Pearl Harbor in a shallow dive to a height of 3500 m, Lt Cdr Takahashi led the dive-bombers from *Shokaku* down the northwest side of Ford Island. His immediate chutai of nine aeroplanes targeted the seaplane base at the southeast corner of the island, while the remaining 17 Type 99s of his command hit Hickam Field, the USAAC's main bomber base on Oahu, southeast of Pearl Harbor.

Takahashi pushed over into his dive at 0755 hrs and dropped the first bomb to fall within Pearl Harbor itself on the seaplane ramp in front of Ford Island's Hangar No 6. Other aeroplanes from his chutai quickly followed with bombs on the seaplanes parked outside, the hangar itself and other base facilities. The prevailing wind from the northeast blew the smoke from this attack southwestward, keeping 'Battleship Row' clear for the torpedo bombers. Of the 33 aeroplanes (mainly from the US Navy's Patrol Wing Two) destroyed or damaged out of a total of 70 on Ford Island, the vast majority were victims of Takahashi's dive-bombers.

Almost simultaneously with the attack on Ford Island, Takahashi's subordinate buntaicho, Lts Masao Yamaguchi and Hisayoshi Fujita, pounced on Hickam. They bombed the hangars and other base facilities, and together with Zero-sen fighters strafed the bombers of the 18th Bombardment Wing on the ground. As at Wheeler, the aeroplanes at Hickam had been parked in neat rows as a precaution against sabotage. Hickam would be hit by several subsequent waves of strafers, including some dive-bombers from the second wave after their attack on ships in the harbour, and by second wave high-level bombers. By the time the IJN aircraft left the area, four B-17Ds, twelve B-18As and two A-20As would lie destroyed at Hickam, with numerous others damaged.

Following their attack on Ford Island and Hickam Field, the *Shokaku* dive-bombers flew to Barbers Point – an initial assembly point on the

The wrecked destroyers USS *Downes* (DD-375) and USS *Cassin* (DD-372) in Drydock No 1 at the Pearl Harbor Navy Yard soon after the end of the Japanese air attack. *Cassin* has capsized against *Downes*. USS *Pennsylvania* (BB-38) is astern, occupying the rest of the drydock. The torpedo-damaged cruiser USS *Helena* (CL-50) is in the right distance, beyond the crane. Visible in the centre distance is the capsized USS *Oklahoma* (BB-37), with USS *Maryland* (BB-46) alongside. Smoke is from the sunken and burning USS *Arizona* (BB-39), out of view behind *Pennsylvania*. USS *California* (BB-44) is partially visible at the extreme left. Two Type 99 dive-bombers from *Soryu* had targeted *Downes* and *Cassin* after they had been unable to line up on *Pennsylvania* (*US Naval Historical Center*)

southwest coast. Some joined Zero-sens in a series of strafing attacks on Marine Corps assets at Ewa Mooring Mast Field en route. They then made their way to the main rendezvous area northwest of Kaena Point, on Oahu's extreme western tip, before heading back to their carrier.

About ten miles northwest of Kaena Point, some of the *Shokaku* dive-bombers came upon one of their opposite number in the new war they had launched this day. *Enterprise* was returning to Pearl Harbor after delivering a dozen F4F-3 Wildcat fighters of VMF 211 to Wake Island, the vessel now being less than a day's sailing from port. Starting at 0615 hrs, while still some 250 miles west of Oahu, *Enterprise* had launched 18 SBD-2/3s to fly a search pattern ahead of the carrier and continue on to land at Ford Island. At around 0833 hrs, one of them, SBD-2 '6-B-3' of VB-6, flown by Ens Manuel Gonzalez, with Radioman 3/c Leonard J Kozelek in the rear seat, crossed paths with *Shokaku's* Type 99 Kanbaku.

In the first aerial encounter of the Pacific War between opposing dive-bombers, six Type 99s shot down Gonzalez and Kozelek, who, tragically, thought they had fallen victim ro friendly fire. The *Shokaku* dive-bombers were also to lose one of their own, but to navigational error rather than enemy action. 'EI-239' – the 'Tail-end Charlie' in Lt Fujita's chutai – flown by F 1/c Kunio Iwatsuki, with F 1/c Tetsusaburo Kumakura as observer/commander, lost its way during the return flight. Accurate aerial navigation over water remained a problem in the IJN, and would continue to plague it in coming months.

At 1307 hrs, long after the rest had landed safely back aboard *Shokaku*, Kumakura radioed that they were about to ditch. Refusing to ask for bearings home for fear of revealing Kido Butai's position, the crew apologised instead for their error, which was about to result in the loss of one of His Imperial Majesty's aircraft. With a final 'Tennoheika banzai!' ('Long live the emperor!'), the aircraft and its crew were swallowed up in the vast Pacific Ocean somewhere in the vicinity of N Lat 25 deg 28 min, W Long 157 deg 57 min. This was the first wave's sole dive-bomber loss, although 17 others had returned with combat damage – 13 to *Zuikaku* and four to *Shokaku*.

As the first wave departed Oahu, the second wave approached. The formation neared Kahuku Point from the northeast at 0840 hrs, and Lt Cdr Shimazaki ordered deployment in preparation for combat three minutes later. As the airmen sped south along the

A kanbaku from the second wave, its dive brakes deployed, screams down on Pearl Harbor, having just released its 250 kg ordinary bomb (*NA 80-G-15446 via Mike Wenger*)

An IJN aerial photograph of Pearl Harbor's 'Battleship Row' under attack on the morning of 7 December 1941 (*US Naval Historical Center*)

windward side of Oahu's north shore, they fanned out, the high level Type 97s swinging wide to port and the fighter top cover climbing to starboard. The dive-bombers went straight down the centre, with Lt Cdr Egusa in the lead.

At 0855 hrs came the general attack order from Shimazaki. Egusa and his dive-bombers from *Soryu* crossed the coast directly over Kaneohe. They then continued south and did not turn west for Pearl Harbor until they were along the seaward side of Honolulu. The *Hiryu* dive-bombers, following hard on their heels to starboard, crossed slightly to the west of Kaneohe. The kanbaku from *Kaga* and *Akagi*, trailing on the port side, actually rounded Diamond Head before flying over Honolulu in their approach to Pearl Harbor. The defences had by now been thoroughly alerted, and bursts of anti-aircraft fire peppered the air above the harbour. Thick smoke resulting from the first wave attack obscured many of the warship targets below, making precise aiming extremely difficult, even for the superbly trained kanbaku crews of 1st and 2nd Koku Sentai.

Egusa led his Type 99s in one large, clockwise circuit of the harbour at an altitude of 4000 m, quite unmindful of the flak bursts around them, and gave his order attack order while above Hickam Field at 0902 hrs. With so much smoke in the harbour, Egusa could not get a clear line of sight to a target. He simply followed the strings of tracer fire back to their source, reasoning that they must originate from an active ship down below. He aborted his first dive and set up his attack again, releasing his bomb against the heavy cruiser USS *New Orleans* (CA-32) moored at the Navy Yard on the southeast side of Pearl Harbor. The weapon missed its mark, however, detonating instead between the cruiser and repair ship USS *Rigel* (AR-11), showering *New Orleans* with shrapnel.

Egusa's two wingmen aimed initially for the battleship USS *Pennsylvania* (BB-38) in Drydock No 1 but were unable to line up their attack properly. They switched targets and hit the destroyers USS *Cassin* (DD-372) and USS *Downes* (DD-375) forward of BB-38 in the same drydock, engulfing these smaller vessels in flames. Following the bombing, Egusa's shotai strafed the destroyer USS *Dale* (DD-353) as it headed down the main channel toward the harbour entrance. FPO 1/c Ryo-ichi Takahashi (observer/aircraft commander) and FPO 3/c Satoru Kawasaki (pilot) in the shotai's No 3 aeroplane were hit by flak during this attack and they plunged to their deaths just west of the harbour entrance buoys.

The leader of *Soryu's* second shotai, Lt Michiji Yamashita, with FPO 1/c Norio Nakagawa (pilot), had aimed for the battleship USS *Maryland* (BB-46) but ended up splashing their bomb near the fleet oiler USS *Neosho* (AO-23), which had cast off its moorings in front of *Maryland* and moved into mid-channel, stern first. Yamashita's two wingmen bombed the light cruiser USS *Helena* (CL-50) tied up at 1010 Dock nearby, achieving near misses, but no direct hits. The No 3 aeroplane of FPO 2/c Hideyasu Kuwabara (FPO 3/c Kenji Maruyama/pilot) from this shotai also failed to return. Japanese sources credit anti-aircraft fire from *Helena* with its demise, but it was possibly downed at a later point in the withdrawal.

The third shotai split up to bomb widely separated targets. The leading aircraft of FPO 1/c Noboru Asakura (pilot) and FPO 1/c Kanetsugu Funasaki (observer/commander) claimed a hit on the battleship USS *California* (BB-44), moored off the southern end of 'Battleship Row', while the two wingmen splashed their bombs off the port quarter of the destroyer tender USS *Dobbin* (AD-3) anchored north of Ford Island.

The leader of *Soryu's* second chutai, Lt Masai Ikeda (WO Sakae Terai as observer), hit the starboard side of *Pennsylvania's* boat deck, while the No 2 aeroplane of FPO 1/c Takashi Yamada (pilot) and FPO 1/c Kazuyoshi Fujita (observer/commander) struck the destroyer USS *Shaw* (DD-373) in Floating Drydock No 2. The No 3 near-missed *Helena*.

The second shotai in Lt Ikeda's chutai was short one aeroplane, as the No 2 machine had aborted the mission with engine trouble. Nevertheless, the shotai leader, Lt Moriyuki Koide (FPO 1/c Hiroshi Yamamoto as observer), and his No 3 both dived on, but apparently missed, *California. Soryu's* last dive-bomber shotai split up to attack widely separated targets, but they also failed to score any hits.

When *Hiryu's* dive-bomber leader, Lt Michio Kobayashi, was forced to abort, the second chutai leader, Lt Takashi Nakagawa (WO Toshikatsu Nishihara as pilot), moved into the lead with his chutai. Nakagawa aimed for the light cruiser USS *St Louis* (CL-49), but failed to score a hit. His No 2 also bombed the ships clustered in the Navy Yard with uncertain results, while the No 3 targeted the battleship USS *West Virginia* (BB-48) across the channel, but likewise failed to score. The lead aircraft of the second shotai, commanded by WO Shimematsu Nakayama (FPO 1/c Shizuo Nakagawa as pilot), and his No 2 also bombed the ships in the Navy Yard, but reported uncertain results, their targets obscured by smoke from previous attacks.

Although this concentration of attacks on ships in the Navy Yard failed to score any direct hits, they registered at least one near miss that caused serious flooding in the hull of the light cruiser USS *Honolulu* (CL-48), moored next to *St Louis*.

Smoke from Ford Island as well as a layer of scattered cloud at a height of 1000 m hampered the attack of the second shotai's No 3 aeroplane ('BII-207') of FPO 3/c Tatsuo Itazu (with F 1/c Sumio Kondo as pilot), as he recalled:

'As the smoke cleared momentarily over the channel, our intended target revealed itself to be

*Akagi's* dive-bombers participated in the second wave attack on 'Battleship Row', the vessel's Type 99s being led by Lt Takehiko Chihaya (with FPO 1/c Kiyoto Furuta as his pilot). His bomb, and that of his two wingmen, splashed near the fleet oiler USS *Neosho* (AO-23) (*Author*)

The forward magazine of USS *Shaw* (DD-373) explodes during the second wave attack. To the left of the explosion, *Shaw's* stern is visible at the end of Floating Drydock No 2 (*US Naval Historical Center*)

a mere destroyer. I yelled into the voice tube to my pilot – "Go right! Go right!". Itazu hastily ordered Kondo to reset his sights on the *California* to starboard. Having thus extended their dive, they barely managed to pull out in time, the metal skin on the wings of their Type 99 creasing in protest at the stress loads incurred. 'We flashed past below the level of the main masts and saw a column of smoke and flame rise amidships behind the smoke stack'.

The entire third shotai aimed for the battleship USS *Maryland* (BB-46) moored inboard of the battleship USS *Oklahoma* (BB-37), which had already capsized following attacks by torpedo-bombers in the first wave. The aircraft of the shotaicho, WO Shoro Ishii (FPO 1/c Hiroyasu Kawabata as pilot) and the No 3 made it through, but the No 2 aircraft ('BII-214') of FPO 2/c Isamu Kiyomura (pilot) and FPO 2/c Yoshio Shimizu (observer/commander) was hit by flak and withdrew smoking to the northeast. This aeroplane is believed to have crashed at Aiea Heights.

What had been Lt Kobayashi's lead chutai now followed. As the ranking officer, second shotai leader Lt(jg) Ichiro Shimoda (FPO 1/c Kataru Sumiyoshi as observer) had taken over the chutai lead with his wingmen. Shimoda and his No 2 dived on *Maryland*, while his No 3 joined third shotai leader WO Keijiro Yoshikawa (FPO 1/c Kishichiro Yamada as pilot) and the latter's No 2 in attacking *Helena*. Yoshikawa's No 3 ('BII-233'), manned by FPO 2/c Koreyoshi Toyama (pilot/commander) and F 1/c Hajime Murao (observer), targeted *Pennsylvania* but missed. Kobayashi's two orphaned wingmen dove on the destroyer USS *Helm* (DD-388) outside the harbour, inflicting slight damage with near misses. Observer/commander of the No 3 machine, FPO 3/c Akira Okura, was badly wounded by flak from *Helm*, however.

*Akagi's* dive-bombers approached the harbour from the southeast at an altitude of 3500 m and began a shallow descent as they crossed Honolulu. The bombs of the leader, Lt Takehiko Chihaya (with FPO 1/c Kiyoto Furuta as pilot), and of both his wingmen splashed near the oiler *Neosho*, which was now headed into Southeast Loch. The three Type 99s of the second shotai, led by Lt Shohei Yamada (FPO 1/c Yoshitake Nozaka

One of several Type 99s from the second wave hit by flak going down in flames in the harbour area. Japanese aircrew were amazed at the swiftness of the American response. Like all Japanese aircraft of this period, the Type 99 Carrier Bomber was extremely vulnerable to fire, having no self-sealing fuel tanks or armour protection for its crew (*NA 80-G-32952 via Mike Wenger*)

A Type 99 of the second wave, probably from *Kaga*, pulls up after its dive over the harbour to be captured on film by an American cameraman below (*NA 80-G-15447 via Mike Wenger*)

USS *Nevada* (BB-36) beached and burning after being hit forward by bombs from no fewer than 23 of *Kaga's* 26 Type 99s. Its pilothouse area is discoloured by fires in that vicinity. The harbour tug USS *Hoga* (YT-146) is alongside *Nevada's* port bow, helping to fight fires on the battleship's forecastle. Note the channel marker buoy caught up alongside *Nevada's* starboard side (*US Naval Historical Center*)

This Type 99 from *Kaga* had its tail assembly blown off by flak and crashed in Middle Loch off the port beam of the destroyer-minelayer *Montgomery*. Note the flotation bags deployed from its wings and the dive angle sighting lines painted just below the windscreen (*NA 80-G-33014 via Mike Wenger*)

Note details of the OEG telescopic sight, complete with lens cover, in front of the pilot's windscreen (*Naval History and Heritage Command*)

as observer), unable to line up properly on *Pennsylvania*, released their bombs instead on *Shaw* in Floating Drydock No 2. They reported uncertain results, their view obscured by smoke, but at least two of their bombs found their mark. The resulting fires eventually set off the destroyer's forward magazine in a spectacular explosion that blew the ship's bow off.

The entire third shotai, led by WO Toshio Oyama (FPO 2/c Sei-ichi Ota as pilot) was wiped out. Oyama, in 'AI-225', aimed for the seaplane tender USS *Tangier* (AV-8) moored northwest of Ford Island, and scored a near miss. His aeroplane was then hit by flak from several ships and crashed into the No 1 crane onboard the seaplane tender USS *Curtiss* (AV-4). Oyama's two wingmen also fell to anti-aircraft fire in the harbour area. One of them achieved a hit on *Curtiss*, but came down off Beckoning Point, while the other, having targeted a vessel further east, crashed in a cane field west of Aiea.

Lt Zenji Abe (WO Chiaki Saito as observer), leading *Akagi's* second chutai, ordered his unit into the attack while still over Honolulu. As the eight Type 99s of his command trailed behind him at 100 m intervals, they picked up speed in their shallow descent toward the harbour. At 2500 m, with Ford Island before him, Abe banked sharply left and pushed over into his dive, followed by his two wingmen. Abe initially targeted USS *Arizona* (BB-39), which was the starboard-most vessel in 'Battleship Row', but quickly saw that it had already been destroyed. He flew over to the opposite side of Ford Island and targeted the light cruiser USS *Raleigh* (CL-7) instead, as did both his wingmen. One of the three bombs scored a hit.

The six kanbaku of the second and third shotai all aimed for *Maryland*. They were unsure of their results because of smoke, but optimistically claimed five hits. Despite this concentration of effort against *Maryland* by both them and previous Type 99s, the battleship was hit by only two 250 kg bombs and sustained only slight damage, with just four crewmen being killed.

USS *Nevada* (BB-36) was not so lucky. The only battleship to get underway during the attack, it pulled alongside 1010 Dock in a

The tailless Type 99 was hauled up on Ford Island for inspection. The radio antenna atop the observer's cockpit has been broken off by the impact of the flak hit on the tail. The aeroplane's commander, FPO 3/c Naga-aki Asahi, drowned himself in the observer's rear cockpit when approached by civilian contractors in a boat, while the pilot, FPO 3/c Noboru Sakaguchi, was shot in the water by a sailor from a navy boat sent out by *Montgomery* (*NA 80-G-33017 via Mike Wenger*)

The shattered cockpit of the Middle Loch Type 99 (*Naval History and Heritage Command*)

bid for the open sea. However, the vessel was spotted by Lt Saburo Makino (WO Sueo Sukida as observer), *Kaga's* senior kanbaku buntaicho, who had been circling above the harbour with his three chutai of dive-bombers, awaiting his turn to attack. Seeing a golden opportunity to bottle up the entire fleet by sinking the battleship in mid-channel, he led no fewer than 23 of *Kaga's* 26 kanbaku against the warship, pummelling it. BB-36 bravely steamed down-channel toward the harbour entrance. Most of the bombs missed, but five struck home. The *Kaga* dive-bombers continued their attack for some minutes after *Nevada's* crew, realising the danger, ran the vessel aground off Hospital Point.

Only the three aeroplanes of the third shotai from Lt Shoichi Ogawa's second chutai went after other targets, dropping their bombs on *Maryland* and *West Virginia* along 'Battleship Row'.

At least two of *Kaga's* dive-bombers fell to anti-aircraft fire over the harbour. Ogawa's No 3, commanded by FPO 3/c Naga-aki Asahi (observer) and piloted by FPO 3/c Noboru Sakaguchi, crashed in Middle Loch off the port beam of destroyer-minelayer USS *Montgomery* (DM-17). The crew of two boats sent out to investigate became the first Americans to witness Japan's harsh warrior code in action. For the men of the imperial armed forces, surrender was not an option. Asahi calmly removed his flight helmet, goggles and life jacket and drowned himself as a civilian boat approached, while Sakaguchi, thrashing in the water, was shot by one of the men in a boat sent out from the *Montgomery*.

Another Type 99 seen to crash on Waipio Peninsula was probably that of FPO 1/c Kazuyoshi Kuwabata (observer/commander) and FPO 3/c Shigenori Onikura (pilot) from Lt Shoichi Ibuki's third chutai.

Following their bombing attack, many of the second wave Type 99s went on to strafe Hickam and Ewa fields, before retiring northward. After their strafing of the destroyer *Dale*, Lt Cdr Egusa's No 2, FPO 1/c Tadashi Endo (observer/commander) and FPO 2/c Takeo Yamazaki (pilot), encountered one of the B-17Es that had flown in from California. As the four-engined bomber came in on its final approach to Hickam Field, Yamazaki made two passes at it with his twin, forward-firing 7.7 mm guns, but to no effect. He eventually formed up with FPO 1/c Funasaki's third shotai and headed back to *Soryu* without encountering any more enemy aircraft.

A handful of USAAC fighter pilots were by now rising to the challenge of this devastating surprise attack, having raced in their cars from the carnage at Wheeler to the small airstrip at Haleiwa, on the leeward side of Oahu's north shore, which so far remained untouched by the Japanese. 2Lts George S Welch and Kenneth M Taylor of the 47th Pursuit Squadron/15th Pursuit Group were the first to arrive, and they took off in two P-40Bs. Hard on their heels in a second car came squadronmates 2Lts John L Dains and Harry W Brown, together with the squadron executive officer, 1Lt Robert J Rogers, harassed by a strafing Type 99.

Dains managed to take off in a P-40B before the dive-bomber came over to strafe the airstrip, this being the only time that Haleiwa was attacked. Dains gave chase and apparently pursued the Type 99 along much of the north shore, finally shooting it down into the sea off Kaaawa, on the windward side of the island. It is conjectured that his victim may have been POs Kuwabara and Maruyama from *Soryu*.

Meanwhile, Lts Welch and Taylor had flown south, finally meeting Japanese aircraft over Ewa Mooring Mast Field. Here, several Type 99s were busy strafing the field. Welch attacked the kanbaku of F 1/c Yasuhiko Mizuno (observer/commander) and F 1/c Kazunari Fuchigami (pilot), the No 3 wingman in WO Ishii's shotai from *Hiryu*, and claimed it destroyed. This aeroplane did indeed have its left wing tank punctured, but the dive-bomber returned to its carrier. Taylor, meanwhile, had latched onto another *Hiryu* dive-bomber, believed to be crewed by Toyama and Murao, and shot it down just inland from Ewa Beach.

George Welch now got onto the tail of Zenji Abe's No 2 aircraft from *Akagi*, commanded by FPO 2/c Michiji Utsuki (observer) and piloted by FPO 2/c Hajime Goto. Fire from Utsuki's rear 7.7 mm gun caused Welch to pull up abruptly with smoke pouring from his aeroplane, prompting the Japanese to claim him as a kill. But Ken Taylor, coming up behind Welch, fatally struck Utsuki with his fire and shot the dive-bomber down just offshore from Barbers Point. PO Goto survived the crash and waded ashore carrying Utsuki, who was either mortally wounded or already dead. Goto buried his observer on the beach and remained at large in the Barbers Point area until Tuesday, 9 December, when he was finally killed by US Army personnel from the 55th Coast Artillery Regiment.

Witnesses to the demise of Utsuki and Goto were observer Lt(jg) Keizo Obuchi (who changed his name to Jiryu Motojima postwar) and his pilot FPO 1/c Yoshiharu

Lt Zenji Abe stands proudly in front of *Akagi's* 'AI-202' at Iwakuni air base in early January 1942 following his safe return from the attack on Pearl Harbor. Note the lack of red flash markings on the wheel covers of the Type 99s. Evidence indicates that *Akagi's* 2nd Chutai dive-bombers did not carry these markings until they departed Japan for Operation *R* later in the month (*Zenji Abe via Lambert/Lansdale*)

Tanaka. Obuchi was the second shotai leader in Lt Abe's chutai, and he and his two wingmen were circling off Barbers Point waiting for other aeroplanes to assemble at this time.

The aircraft ('AI-208') of his No 3 crew – FPO 2/c Michiji Kawai (observer/commander) and FPO 3/c Tokuji Iizuka (pilot) – was leaking fuel from its right wing tank, which had been hit by flak during the dive-bombing attack on *Maryland*. Kawai and Iizuka were blithely unaware of the damage until Obuchi wrote a message on his hand-held chalkboard ordering them to return immediately to their carrier. They gladly complied and made it back to *Akagi* on their own, but hit the crash barrier on landing, bending the rear fuselage at right angles. The wrecked machine, however, was brought back to Japan and not thrown overboard.

Alone or in small groups, some having first assembled at the preliminary rendezvous point off Barbers Point, the aeroplanes of the second wave made their way to the main post-strike rendezvous area bearing 340 degrees, 20 miles out from Kaena Point. Lt Makino, *Kaga's* kanbaku leader, led a dozen dive-bombers north, but decided to strafe Wheeler Field along the way. Lts Welch and Taylor had withdrawn to Wheeler in order to rearm following their combat over Ewa, and they took off in the teeth of Makino's attack. As Ken Taylor aimed for one of the *Kaga* Type 99s, Makino, attempting to come to his subordinate's aid by circling round onto Taylor's 'six o'clock', slightly wounded the American pilot (and damaged the P-40B) with his forward guns.

Moments later, however, George Welch came up behind Makino and shot him down just outside the base gate at Wahiawa. A graduate of the IJN's Naval Academy Class 60 of 1933, Saburo Makino became the senior-most officer lost by the Japanese during the Pearl Harbor attack.

With his tail now clear, Taylor focused on the *Kaga* dive-bomber in his sights and shot it down north of Wahiawa. He then flew north and claimed another *Kaga* Type 99 out at sea north of Oahu, its crew opting to 'self-destruct' after having suffered heavy damage at Taylor's hands.

Following the brief strafing at Haleiwa, Lts Harry Brown and Bob Rogers took off in P-36s and came upon the main Japanese rendezvous off Kaena Point. They attacked a dive-bomber and claimed it shot down, but this aeroplane did not immediately crash.

Aboard *Kaga*, just prior to take-off, Lt Makino's No 3 had been grounded with engine trouble. Makino ordered third shotai leader WO Yonekichi Nakajima to give up his No 2, FPO 2/c Fumio Hirashima (pilot/commander) and FPO 3/c Toshiaki Bando (observer) as replacement for Makino's No 3.

According to Nakajima's eyewitness testimony, he saw Hirashima and Bando approach his aircraft off Kaena Point waving their hands, glad to see that their usual shotaicho was safe. Their own aircraft, however, had been damaged and was leaking fuel, probably as a result of encountering Brown and Rogers. Heedless of the danger this posed, Hirashima throttled back to fly formation with Nakajima. Exhaust flames flared up from the change in throttle setting and instantly ignited the fuel vapour, engulfing the kanbaku in a ball of fire. Nakajima frantically gestured to them to try for Niihau Island, the

Lt Saburo Makino, *Kaga's* senior dive-bomber leader, became the senior-most Japanese officer lost in action on 7 December 1941 when he was shot down by future ace 2Lt George Welch over Wheeler Field (*Gordon Prange Collection via Mike Wenger*)

The crash site of Makino's aircraft, which hit a house at Wahiawa, just outside the Wheeler Field gate. Makino and his observer, WO Sueo Sukida, both perished (*1115C-127009 via Mike Wenger*)

designated emergency landing zone to the west, but to no avail. As Nakajima watched helplessly, Hirashima and Bando plunged to their deaths, leaving a column of oily black smoke on the sea.

Dive-bomber crews from *Akagi* had been given the task of collecting all remaining stragglers, with orders to circle off Kaena Point for 30 minutes before heading home. When Lt(jg) Obuchi reached the rendezvous point together with his No 2, he dutifully extended his loop antenna from the underside of his aircraft and sent out a homing signal as he circled. But nobody showed up, all aircraft apparently having gone on ahead. The two *Akagi* Type 99s headed northeast and soon overtook the shotai from *Hiryu* commanded by Lt(jg) Shimoda, Obuchi's naval academy classmate. These five then caught up with *Hiryu*'s Lt Nakagawa, who was leading WO Yoshikawa and the latter's No 2, together with PO Itazu from his own second shotai.

As they headed further north, these nine kanbaku encountered, and briefly attacked, PBY-5 '14-P-2' from VP-14, flown by Ens Otto F 'Freddie' Meyer Jr. They claimed the flying boat shot down, but had in fact inflicted only minimal damage. Continuing north at an altitude of 2000 m, they next ran into a B-17E hugging the waves and gave chase. This was another of the bombers that had flown in from the West Coast that morning, this machine (flown by 1Lt Frank P Bostrom) hailing from the 88th Reconnaissance Squadron/7th Bomb Group. The kanbaku crews got a first-hand taste of the ruggedness of the Flying Fortress as repeated passes failed to bring down the four-engined bomber. After a chase of some 11 minutes, however, they managed to shoot out its two left engines and forced it down onto a tiny airstrip adjacent to Kahuku Golf Course near the northern tip of Oahu.

Having loitered longer than was prudent in chasing the two enemy aircraft, Nakagawa's formation hurried north, now concerned about their fuel situation. Kido Butai was 250 miles away. The formation crossed paths with a Zero-sen headed in the opposite direction leaking a vapor trail of fuel. PO Itazu closed his eyes in silent prayer for the unfortunate pilot who had apparently given up hope of reaching a friendly flightdeck in his condition, and was heading back to die facing the enemy. Eight other Zero-sens in good condition, however, eagerly joined Nakagawa's band of dive-bombers, grateful for navigational guidance home. The fate of 17 aircraft and their crews now rested in Lt Nakagawa's hands.

'In a heavy mist, we reached the designated location', recalled Nakagawa, 'but we could not find the fleet'. He then changed course 45 degrees into the wind. 'We flew for five minutes on this heading but saw nothing. We made another 45-degree turn. If we were still unable to find anything now, it would be the end. There was nothing left to do but pray. Then, ever so faintly, I saw the trace of a ship's wake'. The aeroplanes broke formation and dispersed to their respective carriers. Nakagawa's fuel gauge registered 'zero', and as he touched down on *Hiryu* his engine stopped with a bang. Lt(jg) Obuchi's kanbaku was the last aeroplane back aboard *Akagi*. Years later, Obuchi recalled how Vice Adm Nagumo actually came down from the bridge onto the flightdeck and embraced him, saying 'It's good to see you've made it back!'

There was, however, one more dive-bomber still making its lonely way back to the task force. F 1/c Shinsaku Yamakawa (pilot/commander) and his observer F 1/c Katsuzo Nakata, from *Kaga's* third chutai, had decided to head back on their own after finding no one off Kaena Point. Minor engine damage from anti-aircraft fire had caused a slight loss of power, resulting in a slow return flight. Finally, after some two-and-a-half hours, during which Yamakawa had despaired, more than once, of ever finding Kido Butai, they flew over one of their scout submarines and

were heartened to see sailors atop the conning tower waving the Rising Sun flag and cheering them on.

'EII-203', a Type 99 from *Zuikaku*, heads back to its carrier after successfully bombing Wheeler Field. Of the six carriers participating in the Hawaiian operation, *Zuikaku* was the only one not to lose any aircraft. Note the red sword blade-shaped flash on the aeroplane's wheel covers, a marking feature unique to the dive-bombers of 5th Koku Sentai (*Shigeru Nohara*)

Thinking better of their initial decision to ditch next to the submarine, they eventually found *Kaga*. As they passed over the carrier's stern, their fuel-starved engine gave out before the wheels touched the deck. Yamakawa jammed on the brakes as the crash barrier loomed up ahead. The aeroplane nosed over, hitting the flightdeck with its propeller tip. In his excitement over their safe return, Yamakawa had forgotten to deploy his tailhook. The time was 1246 hrs.

The IJN had lost 29 aircraft (not including the *Soryu* Zero-sen from the first wave that ditched on take-off in the two-wave assault), namely five Type 97s, nine A6Ms and fifteen Type 99s. The breakdown of the latter aircraft was as follows – *Shokaku's* lone loss from the first wave, plus two each from *Soryu* and *Hiryu*, four from *Akagi* and six from *Kaga*, in the second wave.

As the aeroplanes returned to their carriers, Nagumo immediately ordered them prepared for another sortie and directed each carrier to report available strength. About a dozen seriously damaged aircraft, half of them dive-bombers, had been pushed overboard to avoid disrupting the tempo of landing operations, but more than 70 percent of the total complement of attack aeroplanes and some 67 percent of fighters were still fit for duty. Dive-bomber strength, however, was below 50 percent. *Shokaku* had 22 Type 99s ready and *Zuikaku* counted 14. The second wave bombers returned with much more damage. *Akagi* reported just two kanbaku operational, *Kaga* had six available and *Soryu* seven. *Hiryu*, lamentably, left no surviving record of individual aeroplane status. Nonetheless, this still amounted to nearly 60 dive-bombers.

Together with more than 100 attack aeroplanes and some 80 fighters, Kido Butai could still launch a force of approximately 240 aircraft, although it was almost certain that an afternoon assault would not be recovered until after dark.

Around 1352 hrs, having amassed all battle reports from his six carriers, Nagumo decided that the primary objective of the operation had been achieved beyond all expectations, and continued retiring northward without following up his earlier order with an actual launch. To this day, historians continue to debate the wisdom of this decision. Fuelled by hindsight, these arguments will never be completely resolved. Kido Butai withdrew at 24 knots, leaving a stunned and furious America in its wake.

# RETURN VOYAGE

Intercepted radio messages confirmed that *Enterprise* was somewhere nearby, but Nagumo did not seek out the American carrier. His only thought was to get outside the range of American air patrols. By dawn on 8 December Kido Butai was 600 miles north of Oahu. That day, Zero-sens maintained combat air patrols (CAP) over the fleet, while attack aeroplanes flew search missions. A course change by Kido Butai left many search aircraft struggling to get back, forcing the fleet to transmit a low-frequency homing signal. Five of them ditched, although the crews were rescued. The seas became rougher as the day progressed, and with the flightdeck pitching, *Soryu* lost a CAP fighter and its pilot overboard in a landing mishap.

That evening, Combined Fleet issued orders to Kido Butai to attack Midway, 1130 miles northwest of Oahu, if circumstances allowed. The seas remained rough, however, particularly from the 10th to the 12th, making refuelling impossible and forcing the ships to slow to as little as nine knots at times. On the night of 14/15 December, with conditions showing little sign of improvement after crossing back over the International Dateline, Nagumo cancelled the Midway strike. Kido Butai had sailed with limited materiel for the Hawaiian operation. Ordnance stores were already getting low, and a more urgent unscheduled errand was about to confront Nagumo's carriers.

On 11 December, Wake Island, 1025 miles west of Midway, had been the scene of the first setback in Japan's timetable of conquest. In their first attempt to capture the atoll, elements of Vice Adm Shigeyoshi Inoue's South Seas Force had been repulsed by US Marine Corps defenders. Planning a renewed effort, Inoue now asked Combined Fleet for carrier support. On 15 December, Combined Fleet ordered Nagumo to assist in the capture of Wake.

In keeping with the prevailing IJN doctrine of deploying massed carrier air power following thorough preparation, Kido Butai proposed that all six carriers first put into Truk, the IJN's fleet anchorage in the central Pacific, on 22 December, and attack Wake after refuelling and conferring in detail with Inoue's command. But South Seas Force insisted on a tighter schedule, with plans already in motion for a 'return match' with the 'Leathernecks' sometime between the 20th and 23rd. This meant that the full strength of Kido Butai could not be used, as the recent rough seas had played havoc with the refuelling schedule.

New plans called for only the two carriers of 2nd Koku Sentai, along with two heavy cruisers and two destroyers, to be detached to support the invasion. These ships split off from the main body of Kido Butai after sunset on 16 December and steamed south. Refuelling on the 17th, they intended to launch their first air strike against Wake five days later.

Meanwhile, back at Pearl Harbor, the US Navy had planned a relief mission to Wake. Task Force 14, commanded by Rear Adm Frank 'Black Jack' Fletcher, was centred around the veteran carrier USS *Saratoga* (CV-3). The vessel, which had only just arrived from San Diego, was underway from Pearl on 16 December and expected off Wake within seven or eight days.

Had Kido Butai's initial proposal for a more measured pace been adopted, the American relief of Wake would surely have occurred.

Following the decision to send only 2nd Koku Sentai, however, Fletcher (given his own refuelling requirements and other delays already incurred) would never have reached the atoll before the Japanese. Nonetheless, a difference of only one or two days in the schedule of either side might well have triggered the first carrier-versus-carrier battle in history barely two weeks after Pearl Harbor. But that was not to be.

On 20 December Japanese intelligence mistakenly interpreted a liaison flight to Wake by a single PBY to be a transfer there of an entire squadron, prompting an urgent request from South Seas Force to move the carrier strike up by one day if possible. *Soryu* and *Hiryu* cranked up to 30 knots and plunged ahead, reaching a point 350 miles from Wake on the 21st. From here, at 0614 hrs, 120 miles farther out than the first wave launch at Pearl Harbor, Rear Adm Tamon Yamaguchi's carriers let fly with 29 dive-bombers and 18 fighters. To insure against loss of direction at such a distance, two Type 97 Attack Aeroplanes provided navigational guidance.

Lt Cdr Egusa led 14 kanbaku from *Soryu*, while Lt Kobayashi, no doubt eager to assuage his frustration at having missed Pearl Harbor, led 15 from *Hiryu*. They made their attack at 0850 hrs, but heavy cloud cover at lower altitude interfered. After an ineffective attack on battery positions, the dive-bombers briefly strafed and departed, having encountered neither anti-aircraft fire nor enemy fighters.

On the 22nd Zero-sens shot down the last two remaining F4F-3s still defending Wake, although three Type 97s were lost in exchange, one crew being rescued. With all enemy aircraft destroyed, a planned second strike with dive-bombers was cancelled.

Still more than 500 miles northeast of Wake, Rear Adm Fletcher spent the entire day of the 22nd refuelling his ships under difficult sea conditions. That night, the vessels of the Japanese invasion fleet approached Wake, and they began landing troops in the early hours of 23 December. News of the landings reached Pearl Harbor during the predawn hours. After much debate at Pacific Fleet headquarters, the relief of Wake was cancelled and Fletcher's ships recalled at 0641 hrs Wake local time. The order was greeted with dismay in Fletcher's command, but there would be no fight with the IJN. Wake's defenders were left to their fate.

After sunrise, Yamaguchi's carriers put a succession of five attack waves over Wake with no losses. *Soryu* provided the first strike from 0716 hrs to 0745 hrs, consisting of six Type 99s and six Zero-sens. *Hiryu* followed with six more dive-bombers and six Zero-sens from 0800 hrs to 0850 hrs, while other kanbaku flew anti-submarine patrols in surrounding waters. The last three strikes were flown by Type 97s. All resistance on the atoll ceased by 1400 hrs, and the last air strike was recovered by 1415 hrs. Mission accomplished, 2nd Koku Sentai headed home.

23 December was also the day that the main body of Kido Butai reached Japan. On the 17th (the day after 2nd Koku Sentai had split off toward Wake) the seas subsided sufficiently for Nagumo's carriers to resume flight operations for the first time since 8 December. Type 99 patrols kept a lookout for enemy submarines, mistaking whales for US submersibles on more than one occasion. Following the successful conclusion of the Wake Island operation, 2nd Koku Sentai returned home on the 29th.

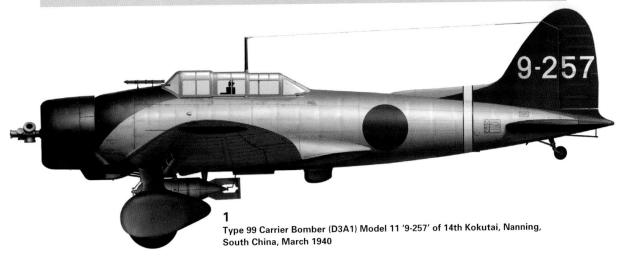

**1**
Type 99 Carrier Bomber (D3A1) Model 11 '9-257' of 14th Kokutai, Nanning,
South China, March 1940

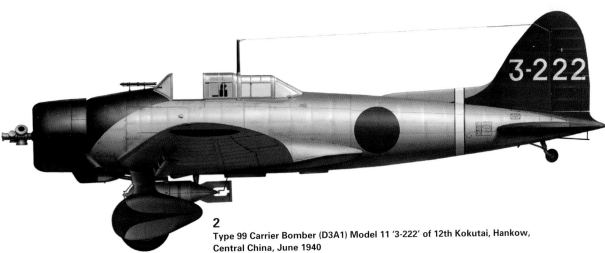

**2**
Type 99 Carrier Bomber (D3A1) Model 11 '3-222' of 12th Kokutai, Hankow,
Central China, June 1940

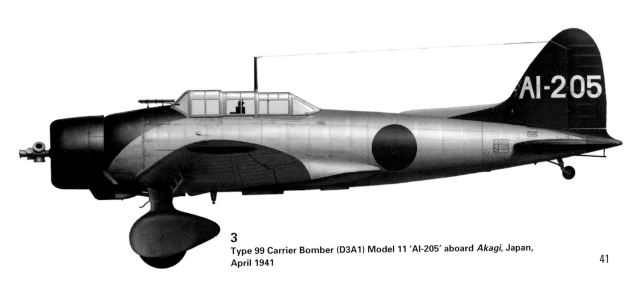

**3**
Type 99 Carrier Bomber (D3A1) Model 11 'AI-205' aboard *Akagi*, Japan,
April 1941

41

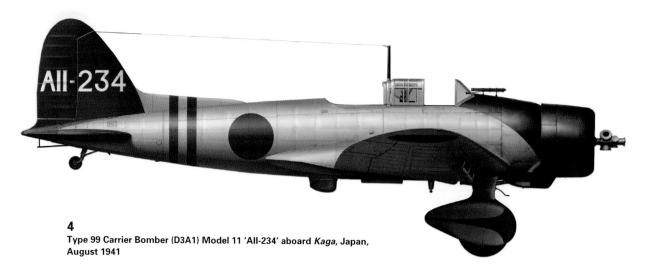

**4**
Type 99 Carrier Bomber (D3A1) Model 11 'AII-234' aboard *Kaga*, Japan,
August 1941

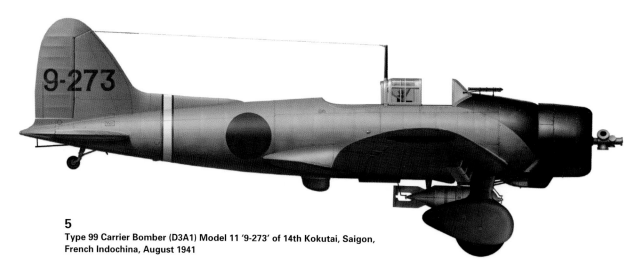

**5**
Type 99 Carrier Bomber (D3A1) Model 11 '9-273' of 14th Kokutai, Saigon,
French Indochina, August 1941

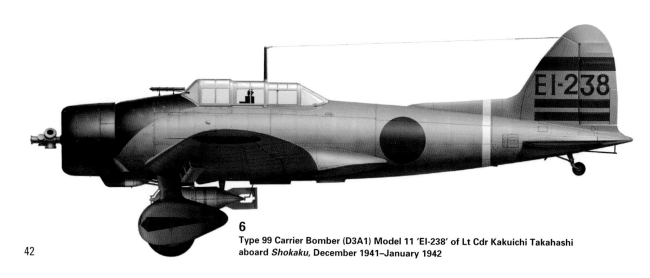

**6**
Type 99 Carrier Bomber (D3A1) Model 11 'EI-238' of Lt Cdr Kakuichi Takahashi
aboard *Shokaku*, December 1941–January 1942

**7**
Type 99 Carrier Bomber (D3A1) Model 11 'BI-231' of Lt Cdr Takashige Egusa aboard *Soryu*, October–December 1941

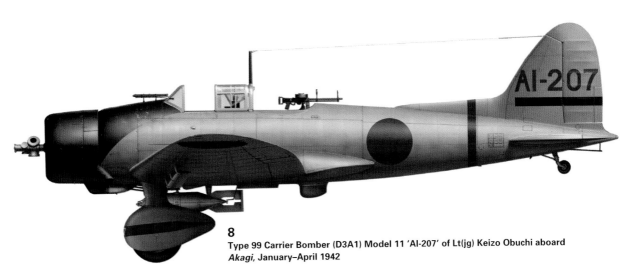

**8**
Type 99 Carrier Bomber (D3A1) Model 11 'AI-207' of Lt(jg) Keizo Obuchi aboard *Akagi*, January–April 1942

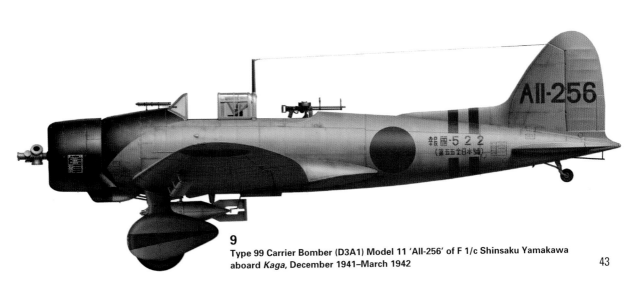

**9**
Type 99 Carrier Bomber (D3A1) Model 11 'AII-256' of F 1/c Shinsaku Yamakawa aboard *Kaga*, December 1941–March 1942

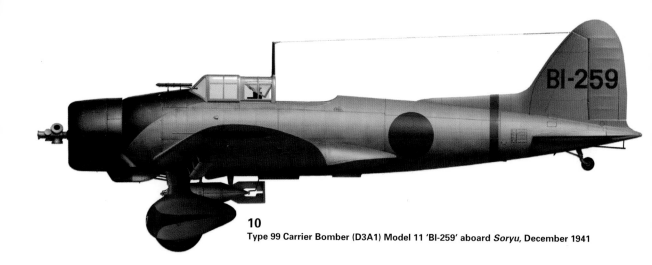

**10**
Type 99 Carrier Bomber (D3A1) Model 11 'BI-259' aboard *Soryu*, December 1941

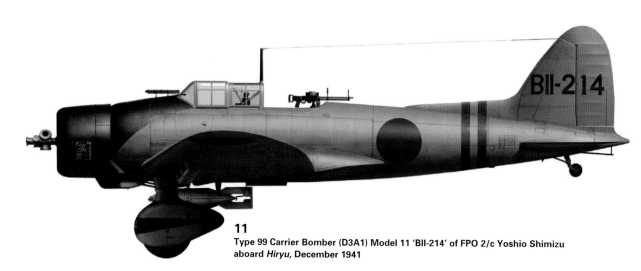

**11**
Type 99 Carrier Bomber (D3A1) Model 11 'BII-214' of FPO 2/c Yoshio Shimizu aboard *Hiryu*, December 1941

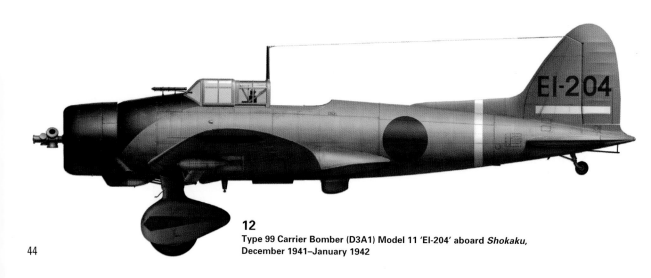

**12**
Type 99 Carrier Bomber (D3A1) Model 11 'EI-204' aboard *Shokaku*, December 1941–January 1942

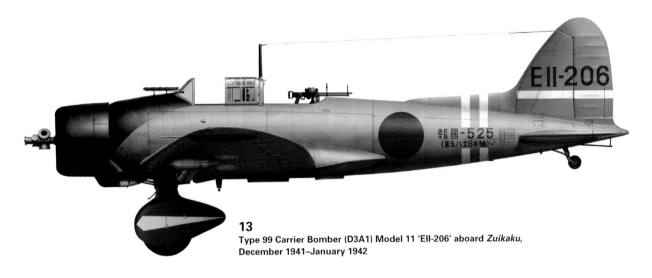

**13**
Type 99 Carrier Bomber (D3A1) Model 11 'EII-206' aboard *Zuikaku*,
December 1941–January 1942

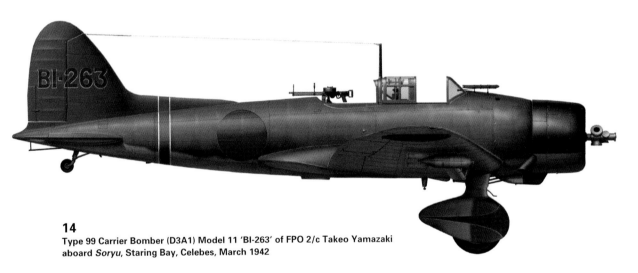

**14**
Type 99 Carrier Bomber (D3A1) Model 11 'BI-263' of FPO 2/c Takeo Yamazaki
aboard *Soryu*, Staring Bay, Celebes, March 1942

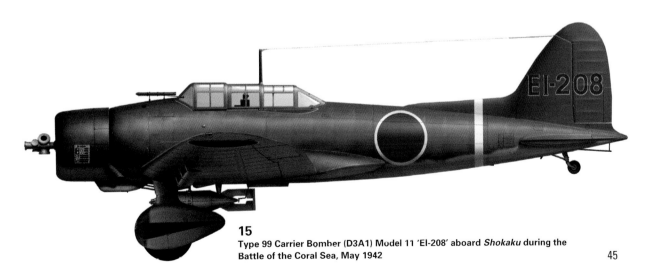

**15**
Type 99 Carrier Bomber (D3A1) Model 11 'EI-208' aboard *Shokaku* during the
Battle of the Coral Sea, May 1942

45

# SOUTHERN ADVANCE

With the battle line of the US Pacific Fleet neutralised, the IJN focused its attention on the conquest of Southeast Asia. Rabaul, in the Bismarck Archipelago, had long been recognised as a key strategic location, and its early capture was a top priority for South Seas Force. Discussions held at Combined Fleet on 24 December 1941 confirmed prewar arrangements for Kido Butai to support South Seas Force following the Hawaiian operation. 1st Koku Sentai (*Akagi* and *Kaga*) and 5th Koku Sentai (*Zuikaku* and *Shokaku*) would support South Seas Force in the capture of Rabaul and Kavieng, codenamed Operation *R*, while 2nd Koku Sentai would come under the direct command of Vice Adm Nobutake Kondo's Southern Force and participate in the main thrust against the Netherlands East Indies.

With personnel rested over the New Year holidays, the bulk of Kido Butai, including *Akagi*, *Zuikaku* and *Shokaku*, left Japan on 8 January 1942 and arrived at Truk on the morning of the 14th (*Kaga* and other supporting vessels followed on the 9th, arriving on the 15th). A raid on Truk by a Royal Australian Air Force (RAAF) Catalina from Kavieng on the 16th while the carriers rode at anchor inflicted only slight damage to shore facilities, but it gave added urgency to the capture of the Bismarcks.

Nagumo's carriers sortied the next day and reached their launch point 200 miles north of Rabaul on the 20th. Delayed by rain and poor visibility, 109 aircraft led by Cdr Fuchida took-off at 1100 hrs (local time). *Akagi* launched 20 and *Kaga* 27 Type 97 Carrier Attack Aeroplanes, while they also provided nine Zero-sens each. *Zuikaku* contributed 19 Type 99s and six Zero-sens, while *Shokaku* sortied 19 Type 99s.

The dive-bombers, under the overall command of Lt Cdr Takahashi, struck port facilities and the only two vessels in Simpson Harbour, the Norwegian freighter *Herstein* and the floating coal bunker, and former liner, *Westralia*. The Type 97s bombed Lakunai airfield and also lent a hand against the *Herstein*, while the Zero-sen escort quickly disposed of three Wirraways from No 24 Sqn RAAF caught in the air over Lakunai – two more crash-landed. The raid cost the Japanese three aircraft. A *Shokaku*

Under overcast skies, 'EII-206' takes off from 5th Koku Sentai flagship *Zuikaku*, probably on 20 January 1942 for the initial strike on Rabaul, New Britain. Note the eight-rayed command flag of Rear Adm Chuichi Hara atop the mainmast behind the bridge. Careful analysis of this well known photograph appears to indicate that the dark colour of the single shotaicho (flight leader) stripe on the tail has been superimposed on the photograph, apparently by a censor's hand, and that the stripe itself was white in reality. The author is grateful to Don Marsh and James F Lansdale for this insight (*Peter C Smith*)

Type 99, heavily damaged by flak, managed to return to the carrier, but crashed during its landing attempt, killing the crew. *Kaga* lost two Type 97s, with one crew being shot down by anti-aircraft fire over Rabaul and the other ditching near the task force and being rescued. With targets so few and opposition so light, a planned second wave strike was cancelled.

On the 21st 1st Koku Sentai raided Kavieng, on New Ireland, with 52 aircraft, *Akagi* providing 18 Type 99s and *Kaga* 16. Each carrier also furnished nine escort Zero-sens. The steel ketch *Induna Star* was disabled and heavy damage done to facilities. 5th Koku Sentai, meanwhile, had steamed southwest, and on the 21st it launched strikes against New Guinea. *Zuikaku* sent 18 Type 97 Attack Aeroplanes, nine Type 99 Bombers and nine Zero-sens against Lae, the fighters also raiding secondary targets at Bulolo and Wau. *Shokaku* launched six Type 97s, six Type 99s and six Zero-sens against Salamaua, and also sent a separate group of nine Type 97s, six Type 99s and six Zero-sens further west to Madang. These raids all faced negligible opposition and suffered no losses, inflicting damage to buildings and destroying a number of aircraft on the ground. Two RAAF Catalinas were also shot down.

On 22 January 1st Koku Sentai returned to Rabaul with 46 aircraft, taking out the gun batteries on Praed Point. *Akagi* sent 18 Type 97s while *Kaga* sent 16 Type 99s. Each carrier provided six Zero-sens. Two kanbaku ditched on return to *Kaga*, but both crews were rescued.

The Japanese went ashore at Rabaul on the 23rd against minimal opposition. All four carriers contributed small patrols of dive-bombers and fighters, providing continuous air cover over the landing area in shifts. The sole loss was a *Kaga* Zero-sen and its pilot, downed by ground fire while strafing Vunakanau airfield.

The carriers of 1st Koku Sentai returned to Truk on 27 January. 5th Koku Sentai joined it on the 29th, but *Shokaku* departed later that same day, bound for drydock in Yokosuka, Japan. She embarked 5th Koku Sentai aircrew deemed in need of further training, including several from sistership *Zuikaku*, along with their aeroplanes. In return, *Shokaku* transferred 18 Type 99s, 14 Type 97s and ten Zero-sens for use by the other carriers.

In stark contrast to the attack on Pearl Harbor, this series of strikes had offered few targets of value. Mitsuo Fuchida would write that the entire operation was akin to wielding an ox blade to chop a chicken.

Tamon Yamaguchi's 2nd Koku Sentai had a similar experience.

Lt Cdr Kakuichi Takahashi's 'EI-238' from *Shokaku* over Rabaul on 20 January 1942. His aircraft sports the three stripes of a hikotaicho (flying group leader) on its tail (*Shigeru Nohara*)

*Soryu* and *Hiryu* sortied from Hashirajima on 12 January, their mission being to attack Ambon, in the Moluccas, in order to provide flank protection for landings at Kendari, on Celebes (Sulawesi), to the west. The carriers reached Palau on the 17th, where they waited for other forces to assemble, and departed on the 21st.

On 24 January, with Japanese forces landing at Kendari, a total of 54 aircraft comprised of

'EI-204', with the single tail stripe of a shotaicho, takes off from *Shokaku* during Operation *R*. The 60 kg bombs under the wings and the absence of any centreline ordnance indicates a routine patrol or a minor strike (*Michael Wenger*)

nine-aeroplane chutai of Type 97s, Type 99s and Zero-sens from each carrier attacked Ambon. No shipping was found and no enemy aircraft encountered. Bombs were dropped on harbour facilities, gun batteries and barracks southwest of the town, and all aeroplanes returned without loss. On the 25th 2nd Koku Sentai withdrew to Davao, in the southern Philippines, which was then being used as a central anchorage by South Seas Force.

Here, on the 27th, each carrier detached nine Zero-sens and nine Type 99 Kanbaku to the newly captured Kendari airfield to operate as a land-based detachment in that area until Ambon was captured during the first week of February. The nine dive-bombers from *Hiryu* flew on to Balikpapan, Borneo, on the 29th. The carriers themselves also departed Davao on the 27th and returned to Palau the next day.

Following the operation, Yamaguchi submitted a proposal that, rather than conducting pre-invasion strikes along the immediate line of advance, attacking the Allied rear at Darwin, in Australia's Northern Territory – a focal point for reinforcements into the East Indies – would prove a more effective use of his carriers' air power projection capabilities.

Precisely how Kido Butai was to be employed following Operation *R* had yet to be decided. Prewar concern that the carriers would have to continue operating in the central Pacific against the US Navy had evaporated with the triumph at Pearl Harbor. Combined Fleet now decided to ensure swift completion of the southern advance by assigning all of Kido Butai to Vice Adm Kondo's Southern Force, and Combined Fleet issued the necessary orders on 31 January. But the very next day, as if in mockery of Combined Fleet's decision, *Enterprise* and USS *Yorktown* (CV-5) hit the Marshalls. *Akagi*, *Kaga* and *Zuikaku*, still at Truk following Operation *R*, went after them, but the 1060-mile distance to the Marshalls was too great and the raiders escaped.

With pursuit cancelled during the evening of 2 February, the three Japanese carriers headed for Palau, joining 2nd Koku Sentai there on the 8th. That day, Combined Fleet issued formal orders assigning Kido Butai to Kondo's Southern Force. However, it was also worried about the prospect of a US carrier raid on Japan itself, so 5th Koku Sentai was detached from Nagumo's command to be stationed in homeland waters. *Zuikaku* left Palau on the 9th and reached Yokosuka on 13 February.

Meanwhile, 2nd Koku Sentai's land-based detachments patrolled Makassar Strait, the waters around Timor and over the Banda Sea in search of enemy aircraft and shipping. On 1 February *Hiryu's* dive-bombers of the Balikpapan detachment attacked two submarines, including the Dutch K-XIV, while on the 4th those of the *Soryu* detachment at Kendari set the merchantman *Van Lansberge* afire with 60 kg bombs and claimed near misses on its minesweeper escorts, HNMS *Jan van Amstel* and HNMS *Pieter de Bitter*. Both detachments withdrew to Peleliu, in the Palaus, on 6 February, ready to re-board their carriers.

Incorporating Rear Adm Yamaguchi's suggestion, Vice Adm Kondo issued orders on 9 February for a major carrier raid on Darwin, timed to coincide with landings at Koepang, on Timor. This was to be followed by an anti-shipping sweep south of Java. The 9th was also the day that *Kaga* scraped its hull against a coral reef while shifting mooring positions in the shallow confines of Palau anchorage. Temporary repairs by the crew, however, would allow the vessel to participate in upcoming operations against Darwin and the sweep south of Java. Kido Butai, now built around the carriers *Akagi*, *Kaga*, *Soryu* and *Hiryu*, sortied from Palau on the 15th and arrived at its launch point 220 miles north-northwest of Darwin on the morning of 19 February.

Starting at 0752 hrs, Nagumo launched the largest carrier air strike since Pearl Harbor. Departing from their usual practice of having vessels alternate the mission roles of aircraft launched, all four carriers contributed fighters, dive-bombers and attack aeroplanes. Cdr Fuchida led a total force of 188 aircraft, *Akagi* contributing 18 Type 97 Attack Aeroplanes and 18 Type 99 Bombers, *Kaga* providing 27 Type 97s and 18 Type 99s, *Soryu* despatching 18 attack aeroplanes and 18 dive-bombers and *Hiryu* sending 18 attack aeroplanes and 17 dive-bombers. Each carrier also contributed nine escort Zero-sens. The dive-bombers began taking off at 0827 hrs, the attack aeroplanes and their escorts having taken off earlier. The latter assembled over Kido Butai and headed out at 0830 hrs, leaving the Type 99s to catch up en route.

During the approach to the target, Zero-sen pilot FPO 1/c Yoshikazu Nagahama from *Kaga* shot down a PBY northwest of Bathurst Island, then, having lost sight of his squadronmates, flew on and opened the

Bathed in brilliant sunshine on the fine morning of 19 February 1942, 'AI-254' is about to take off from *Akagi*, bound for Darwin, Australia. Note that the aeroplane now sports red flashes on the wheel covers. Ship's crew have turned out in large numbers to cheer on the flyers who are about to mount the largest carrier strike since Pearl Harbor. Note the tropical short-sleeved and short-trousered work uniforms of the ship's crew, distinctly different from the full-length winter uniforms worn during the Hawaiian operation. The hammocks of the crew, rolled up and lashed to the bridge as combat protection against splinter damage, remains a feature in the tradition-bound IJN from the days of the turn of the century coal-fired navy (*Shigeru Nohara*)

A nearly head-on shot from the same sequence taken on 19 February 1942. *Akagi* and *Hiryu* were the only carriers in the world ever built with the bridge on the port side, an arrangement that proved less than successful. Another feature unique to *Akagi* was the downward sloping forward flightdeck. Because of this downward angle, the rear half of the flightdeck beyond the bridge is completely hidden from view in this perspective (*Shigeru Nohara*)

assault ahead of schedule between 0937 hrs and 0945 hrs. In an incredible feat of aerial prowess, he shot down four of five P-40E Warhawks from the 33rd Pursuit Squadron (Provisional) (PS(P)) that intercepted him, then strafed two PBYs moored in the harbour. Lt Robert G Oestreicher, the P-40 flight leader and sole survivor of Nagahama's whirlwind assault, later managed to attack two Type 99s from *Soryu*. Both returned, but one ditched with combat damage, the crew being rescued.

Meanwhile, the main attack force deployed into separate groups for the assault as it passed over Melville Island at 0915 hrs, the dive-bombers going into long, line-astern formations and circling upwind as they approached the harbour from the southeast, climbing to an altitude of 5000 m from their approach altitude of 4000 m. Fuchida gave the Type 99 crews the final attack order at 0940 hrs.

The main assault opened with nine Zero-sens from *Soryu* strafing the auxiliary minesweeper HMAS *Gunbar* as it passed through the harbour boom gate at 0957 hrs. Shortly thereafter, the high-level Type 97 Attack Aeroplanes made their bomb runs, targeting ships in the harbour as well as the railway wharf and buildings in town. Then it was the dive-bombers' turn. Visibility was unlimited, with a few layers of scattered cloud – a perfect day for dive-bombing. The Type 99s from *Soryu*, led by Lt Cdr Egusa, bombed the destroyer USS *Peary* (DD-226), as well as the 5952-ton Australian freighter *Neptuna* and the 6891-ton tanker SS *British Motorist*. All three vessels were ultimately sunk following other dive-bombing attacks, the *Neptuna* in a spectacular explosion when munitions in its hold, including 200 tons of depth charges, blew up.

The *Soryu* dive-bombers also claimed another transport sunk and hit an oil storage tank onshore. Lt Kobayashi, leading the dive-bombers from *Hiryu*, went after *Peary* too, while the rest of his two chutai sunk the 12,568-ton US Army Transport (USAT) *Meigs*, by far the biggest ship in harbour, as well as another large transport. They also heavily damaged the American seaplane tender USS *William B Preston* (AVD-7) and two transports. The kanbaku from *Akagi*, led by Lt Chihaya, also helped to sink the *Peary*, and inflicted damage on several transports.

Lt Shoichi Ogawa led the Type 99s from *Kaga*. He had become the vessel's senior dive-bomber leader following the death in action of Lt Saburo Makino at Pearl Harbor. Ogawa was something of a legend within the IJN kanbaku corps. On 18 July 1938, as a young lieutenant, he had flown one of four biplane Type 96 kanbaku from 15th Ku that had made a daring landing on enemy-held Nanchang airfield, in central China. The crews then set several parked aeroplanes alight by hand, after

The 6891-ton tanker SS *British Motorist* burns in Darwin harbour after being attack by Type 99s from *Soryu*. Fires from other vessels hit during the raid, as well as Darwin itself, darken the sky behind the doomed ship (*AWM*)

which they took off again before Chinese troops had time to react to the raid.

Leading *Kaga's* first chutai, Ogawa made for RAAF Station Darwin with six aeroplanes, preceded by escorting Zero-sens from *Akagi*, *Kaga* and *Hiryu*. The fighters quickly shared in the destruction of the five remaining P-40Es of the 33rd PS(P) just as they were taking off from the field, then went down to strafe other aeroplanes on the ground. Ogawa's kanbaku added to the destruction by dropping their 242 kg land bombs on hangars and other facilities. During this attack, third shotai leader WO Katsuyoshi Tsuru and his pilot, FPO 1/c Musashi Uchikado, perished when 'AII-254' was hit by ground fire and crashed 2000 m east of the field. Meanwhile, the three Type 99s of Ogawa's second shotai attacked Darwin Civil Field to the west.

Eight minutes after Ogawa led his chutai against the airfields, the second chutai, headed by Lt Toshio Watanabe – the last formation to make its dive – bombed the *Neptuna* and the 4239-ton Australian freighter *Barossa*, which was damaged and later beached. Other vessels sunk were the Australian cargo ship *Zealandia*, the USAT *Mauna Loa*, the lugger *Mavie* and the supply hulk *Kelat*. Among vessels damaged were the USAT *Admiral Halstead* and the Australian hospital ship *Manunda*, USAT *Portmar* and the Australian coastal trader *Tulagi*, the latter two ships, like the *Barossa*, being beached but later salvaged.

Ninety minutes after Kido Butai's raid, RAAF Station Darwin was bombed by 54 land-based attack aircraft, which did most of the damage there. When both raids were over, the Allies had lost 25 aircraft. In addition to ten USAAC P-40Es and three PBYs, the RAAF lost four Hudsons of No 2 Sqn, two more from No 13 Sqn and a Wirraway of No 12 Sqn that had been under repair in one of two demolished hangars. The USAAF lost an A-24 and a P-40E in the same hangar, an LB-30 on the field and three Beechcraft biplanes, one on Bathurst Island and the other two at Darwin's civilian airfield.

Total Japanese losses came to four aircraft and three airmen – two Type 99s, a Zero-sen from *Hiryu* that crashed on Melville Island with its pilot subsequently captured and a Type 97 from *Kaga* that ditched near the task force with combat damage, the crew being rescued.

The raiders departed shortly after 1030 hrs, leaving a scene of utter devastation behind them. During the return flight, the Japanese spotted a vessel 100 miles north of Darwin. After refuelling and rearming back aboard the carriers, nine dive-bombers each from *Soryu* and *Hiryu*, armed with 250 kg ordinary bombs, were sent to deal with it at 1436 hrs. This was the 3200-ton Philippine freighter *Don Isidro*, which the Type 99s found off Cape Fourcroy, along the southwest coast of Bathurst Island. Led by Lt Masai Ikeda, the bombers from *Soryu* attacked it between 1626 hrs and 1642 hrs, leaving the vessel adrift after scoring five direct hits.

Meanwhile, the kanbaku from *Hiryu*, led by Lt Michiji Yamashita (transferred from *Soryu* after Pearl Harbor), found the 2600-ton US freighter *Florence D*. They sank the ship with two to four hits and five near misses. All aeroplanes were back aboard by 1830 hrs.

Kido Butai now withdrew to Staring Bay, in the Celebes, arriving there on the 21st, while its air groups landed at Kendari, just northwest of the bay. Four days later, on 25 February, the fleet sailed again, this time to sweep the seas south of Java to hunt down Allied ships fleeing the imminent fall of that island.

In the early morning of 1 March, as Kido Butai steamed south-southeast of Christmas Island, the 8082-ton Dutch freighter *Modjokerto* was sunk by gunfire from Nagumo's attendant destroyers and the heavy cruiser *Chikuma*. Later that morning a tanker was spotted, prompting a sortie at 1125 hrs by Lt Watanabe's chutai of nine Type 99s from *Kaga*. Their target, the 14,800-ton USS *Pecos* (AO-6) put up a stiff fight, gamely dodging all 250 kg ordinary bombs aimed at it except the last, delivered by Shinsaku Yamakawa. Despite the vessel's weak defensive armament of two three-inch anti-aircraft guns, two 0.50-cal and four 0.30-cal machine guns, *Pecos* paid Yamakawa back, puncturing his oil tank with a well placed shot. Yamakawa managed to return to *Kaga*, but he had a tough time making his landing due to his windscreen and goggles being smeared with oil.

*Soryu* had also despatched nine kanbaku some ten minutes after *Kaga*, but even after this second attack, the tanker's reserve buoyancy kept her stubbornly afloat. A chutai from *Hiryu* was called out next at 1345 hrs. These nine dive-bombers finally scored several telling hits between 1425 hrs and 1450 hrs, with help from nine *Akagi* Type 99s that made a final attack shortly thereafter. But, in its death throes, defensive fire from *Pecos* scored again. The kanbaku of Tatsuo Itazu from *Hiryu* was hit in the fuselage fuel tank. There was no explosion and no external leakage of fuel, but an internal leak caused petrol to collect inside the fuselage. When Itazu's pilot on this mission, FPO 2/c Kozo Ikeda, throttled back just before landing on *Hiryu*, an exhaust spark ignited the volatile liquid, engulfing the aeroplane in flames. Itazu and Ikeda scrambled out as soon as their tailhook caught a wire. Deckcrew rushed up with fire extinguishers, but the gasoline-fed flames could not be snuffed out and Itazu's 'BII-216' was pushed off the stern.

The day's drama was not yet done. Later that afternoon, an enemy warship was discovered trailing behind the task force. Nagumo ordered his battleships and cruisers to sink it, but their long-range gunnery proved embarrassingly ineffective as their target, the destroyer USS *Edsall* (DD-219) changed course frequently, laid smoke and fired torpedoes in a desperate bid for survival. The kanbaku were ordered to assist, *Kaga* launching eight at 1630 hrs, *Soryu* despatching nine others soon after and nine *Hiryu* dive-bombers also taking part. They scored numerous hits and near misses, leaving *Edsall* dead in the water. The battleships *Hiei* and *Kirishima* and heavy cruisers *Tone* and *Chikuma* now closed in, and with a prodigious expenditure of shells literally blew the old 'four-piper' out of the water. Perhaps no more than eight of *Edsall's* crew survived the sinking. All would later perish as prisoners of the Japanese.

On 5 March Cdr Fuchida led a total of 149 aircraft in two waves against the port of Tjilatjap, now the sole remaining point of evacuation from Java. The first wave consisted of 45 horizontal bombers from 1st Koku Sentai, while the dive-bomber contingent, led by Lt Cdr Egusa, came from 2nd Koku Sentai – 16 Type 99 Bombers from *Soryu* and 17 from *Hiryu*. Fighter escort was provided by nine Zero-sens each from *Akagi* and *Kaga*. The second wave was made up entirely of aeroplanes

'33-203' of the 33rd Ku in flight over eastern Java during the early summer of 1942. One of several garrison units activated to patrol the newly conquered territories of Southeast Asia, the 33rd was based at Surabaya, on Java, and equipped with eight Type 99s and eight Type 97s. It was also the only unit to operate the rare, fixed undercarriage, Mitsubishi Type 97 Mark 2 Carrier Attack Aircraft (B5M1) overseas (*Shigeru Nohara*)

A flight of Type 99s from the 35th Ku in mid-1942. Note that '35-201', furthest from the camera, carries a single tail stripe. Usually the mark of a shotaicho, it may denote the leader of the entire squadron in this case, given the small size of the unit. Based at Makassar, on Celebes, the 35th had eight Type 99s on strength (*Shigeru Nohara*)

from 2nd Koku Sentai, these being 18 horizontal bombers from *Soryu* and 17 from *Hiryu*, with each carrier providing nine escorting Zero-sens. The dive-bombers of 1st Koku Sentai did not take part, being held back in case any choice targets were found at sea.

While the Type 97s devastated the town, the Type 99s attacked shipping in the harbour. They sank the new Dutch minelayer *Ram* being constructed there, as well as at least five merchant ships – the 4819-ton *Barentz*, the 1187-ton *Pasir* and three others of under 1000 tons (*Tohiti*, *Canopus* and *Rohan*). They also damaged nine other vessels, including the 1594-ton *Sipora*, these ships all being scuttled to prevent their use by the Japanese. There was no aerial opposition, and all aeroplanes returned without loss. Including destruction wrought by Takao Ku land attack aeroplanes the previous day, Tjilatjap harbour was now the graveyard for some 23 sunken ships.

On the 7th a chutai of nine dive-bombers from *Soryu* sank the 9278-ton Dutch liner *Poelau Bras*. The Dutch command on Java surrendered on 9 March, and Kido Butai returned to Staring Bay on the 11th.

Ever since departing Palau in mid-February, *Kaga* had managed to keep pace with the task force. But now a re-inspection of its hull at Staring Bay caused concern over the vessel's participation in upcoming operations into the heart of the Indian Ocean. With 5th Koku Sentai ordered to rejoin Nagumo's command, *Kaga* departed Staring Bay on the 15th bound for permanent repairs in the homeland.

Having conquered the Philippines, British Malaya and the Netherlands East Indies, Japan now held the vast natural resources of Southeast Asia firmly in its grip. Back on 1 February 1942, in anticipation of a successful conclusion to these campaigns, the IJN had activated five small air units to form part of the garrison force for this sprawling new territory soon to be added to the empire. These were the 31st, 32nd 33rd, 35th and 40th Ku. Each had no more than a chutai of aircraft to be used for patrol purposes.

The 31st Ku, equipped with eight Type 99 Carrier Bombers, was stationed at Nichols Field on the outskirts of Manila, in the Philippines. The 32nd was purely a floatplane unit, and the remaining three kokutai awaited the successful conclusion of operations along the Malay Barrier prior to being assigned to their respective stations on 10 March. The 33rd went to Surabaya, on Java, the 35th to Makassar, in the Celebes, and the 40th to Singapore, with actual deployment taking place during subsequent weeks. 35th Ku, like the 31st, was equipped entirely with Type 99s, while the 33rd and the 40th had a combination of Type 99 Bombers and Type 97 Attack Aircraft.

For the most part, life for these garrison units proved to be a monotonous routine of anti-submarine patrols, convoy escort and training, but not so for the 31st Ku in the Philippines. With its flight echelon led by Lt Sadamu Takahashi (late of 14th Ku), the unit quickly found itself battling remnant US and Filipino forces still stubbornly holding out in the hope of relief from America. From February to early May, the Type 99s of the 31st were kept busy searching for suspected blockade runners among the islands, as well as occasionally bombing targets on Bataan, Corregidor and the other smaller fortified islands in Manila Bay. Two kanbaku were lost to anti-aircraft fire during this period. Following formal surrender of American and Filipino forces on 6 May, the 31st operated from Cebu, in the central Philippines, later that month, and subsequently established a detachment at Davao from July onward.

Although Japan had now achieved its main objectives, the war was far from over. In support of forthcoming operations to invade Burma and the Andaman Islands, Imperial Headquarters and Combined Fleet had formally decided on 14 February to undertake an operation to seek out and destroy the Royal Navy in the Indian Ocean, code-named Operation *C*. Consequently, on 3 March, Adm Yamamoto decided to order 5th Koku Sentai to rejoin Kido Butai with an effective date of the 5th. Once again, however, US carrier activity upset his schedule.

On 4 March *Enterprise* raided Marcus Island, only 998 miles southeast of Tokyo, raising the spectre of an attack on Japan itself in the near future. *Zuikaku* sortied from Kure on the 5th in pursuit, but with no further word of the American task force, it put into Yokosuka next day. *Zuikaku* departed again on 7 March, now joined by sister ship *Shokaku* recently out of dry dock, and set out to rejoin Kido Butai once more. On the 10th, however, intercepted American radio traffic indicated possible enemy activity northeast of Wake Island. 5th Koku Sentai changed course in the Philippine Sea on the 11th in a renewed effort to intercept the Americans, but the radio reports ultimately proved to be a false alarm.

On the 13th Kido Butai reported its intention to depart Staring Bay on 21 March, with plans to attack Ceylon (Sri Lanka) on or about 1 April. But the fuel expended by 5th Koku Sentai in its wild goose chase forced it back to Yokosuka on the 16th to refuel. It departed again the next day, finally arriving at Staring Bay on 24 March.

While the fleet lay at anchor in Staring Bay, the airmen of Nagumo's task force took advantage of the two weeks spent ashore at Kendari in training, incorporating lessons learned in combat since December. On 24 March, the air groups from *Akagi*, *Soryu* and *Hiryu* wheeled, climbed and dived over the ships in Staring Bay in a combined exercise lasting two-and-a-half hours. Having just arrived that same day, the airmen from *Zuikaku* and *Shokaku* did not take part. They had been training hard back in Japan, however.

When Kido Butai finally sailed from Staring Bay on 26 March, it was, without doubt, the most formidable concentration of naval air power on the surface of the planet.

# ZENITH IN THE INDIAN OCEAN

26 March was also the day that Vice Adm Sir James Somerville took command of the British Eastern Fleet at Colombo, in Ceylon. Composed of five battleships, three aircraft carriers, seven cruisers and 14 destroyers, this fleet appeared formidable on paper. But of the battleships, only HMS *Warspite* had been modernised, the others being of antiquated World War 1 vintage. Among the cruisers, only *Cornwall* and *Dorsetshire* were heavy cruisers. Of the aircraft carriers, *Indomitable* and *Formidable* were state-of-the-art ships, but *Hermes* was an old, small vessel without the unique armoured flightdeck of newer British designs. Above all, their strike aircraft – Albacore and Swordfish biplanes – were markedly inferior to those of their IJN adversary.

Somerville divided his ships into two groups. The faster, more modern vessels comprised Force 'A' under his direct command, while the rest made up Force 'B' to act in a supporting role. One advantage enjoyed by the British was radar, a device that the IJN had yet to deploy operationally. Somerville felt that his best hope of successfully engaging the Japanese was in a night torpedo attack with his ASV radar-equipped strike aircraft. On 28 March he received news that the IJN was expected to raid Ceylon on or about 1 April – an accurate assessment of Kido Butai's original schedule. But Allied intelligence had failed to note the subsequent delay in the Japanese timetable. Somerville searched in vain for the enemy fleet for several days, and on 4 April put in for refuelling at the Eastern Fleet's new anchorage at Addu Atoll in the Maldive Islands – a secret base the existence of which the IJN was completely unaware.

Nagumo's fleet had completed refuelling at sea on 3 April and closed on Ceylon from the southeast. It was spotted on the afternoon of the 4th by a Catalina of No 413 Sqn RCAF, which was promptly forced down onto the sea by Zero-sens, but not before it had managed to transmit a contact report via the clear frequency, duly monitored by friend and foe alike. Surprise was now gone, but, at the urging of his staff, Nagumo decided to proceed with an attack on Colombo as planned. At Addu, Somerville made efforts to raise steam with all due haste, finally departing at midnight with Force 'A', leaving Force 'B' to follow.

At 0600 hrs, in the predawn darkness of Easter Sunday, 5 April, Nagumo's carriers began launching a total of 53 Type 97 Attack Aircraft (17 from *Akagi* and 18 each from *Soryu* and *Hiryu*), 38 Type 99 Bombers (19 each from *Zuikaku* and *Shokaku*) and 36 Zero-sen fighters (nine each from *Akagi, Soryu, Hiryu* and *Zuikaku*). With the task force having been spotted the previous day, the Type 99s from *Akagi, Soryu* and *Hiryu* and the torpedo-armed Type 97s from *Zuikaku* and *Shokaku* were held in reserve in case Somerville's fleet was met at sea.

'AI-207', the aircraft of Lt(jg) Keizo Obuchi (a shotaicho from *Akagi*), begins its take-off roll during Operation *C* – the Indian Ocean raid of April 1942. This photograph was probably taken on 5 April 1942 when *Akagi* dive-bombers participated in the sinking of the British heavy cruisers *Cornwall* and *Dorsetshire* (*Michael Wenger*)

For the fifth time since Pearl Harbor, Mitsuo Fuchida led the attack force of 127 aircraft in the observer's seat of *Akagi's* lead Type 97. Zero-sens sweeping ahead of the main formation made short work of six Swordfish of 788 Naval Air Squadron (NAS) that were caught in the air over the harbour as they headed for Ratmalana, Colombo's main airfield to the southeast. As the main Japanese formation arrived over the harbour, Fuchida gave the attack order at 0745 hrs.

Led by Kakuichi Takahashi, *Shokaku's* Type 99s went after shipping in the harbour. The previous day's warning had cleared the area of all vessels able to get underway, but two destroyers, several naval auxiliaries and 21 merchantmen still remained. Takahashi targeted the 11,198-ton armed merchant cruiser HMS *Hector*, the largest ship present. From 3000 m, with his wingmen in tow, he dived at 0750 hrs and scored a hit in the ship's engine room.

Following Takahashi's command shotai of three aeroplanes came Lt Masao Yamaguchi's 1st chutai of nine, then Lt Hisayoshi Fujita's 2nd chutai of seven. They left *Hector* sinking after scoring four hits, and also damaged the 5805-ton submarine depot ship *Lucia*. Their score would likely have been higher had it not been for the heavy layers of cloud that greatly interfered with accurate aiming. Lt(jg) Iwakichi Mifuku, leading the second shotai in Yamaguchi's chutai, aborted his attack twice before finally managing to drop his 250 kg ordinary bomb on his third dive.

While the dive-bombing was still in progress, the kanbaku were attacked by five Hurricane IIBs of No 258 Sqn RAF, which had scrambled from their makeshift airfield at the Colombo Racecourse. There was also intense flak. When Lt Fujita pulled out of his dive, his Type 99 was leaking petrol from a ruptured fuel tank. Following just minutes after the dive-bombers, the high-level Type 97s concentrated their attack on port facilities. They also sank the destroyer HMS *Tenedos* and damaged the merchant ship *Benledi* with their 800 kg bombs.

Meanwhile, dive-bombers from *Zuikaku* (led by Akira Sakamoto), with a mixture of land and ordinary bombs, had continued south along the coast. Fourteen of them turned inland for Ratmalana, while five bombed, but missed, the tanker *British Sergeant* in the harbour. Twenty-one Hurricane IIBs of No 30 Sqn RAF and six Fulmars (three each from 803 and 806 NASs) scrambled from Ratmalana when the Japanese were seen approaching the field. Aided by heavy cloud cover, the first few that scrambled managed to bounce the *Zuikaku* Type 99s before bombs were dropped. Sakamoto's lead chutai of ten lost four aeroplanes in quick succession, while Lt Tamotsu Ema, leading the second chutai of nine, lost his No 3 to the British fighters. Thus distracted, and hampered by cloud cover, the *Zuikaku* dive-bombers did minimal damage to the airfield.

As the Type 99s from *Shokaku* reassembled at 0820 hrs and withdrew, the fuel leak in Lt Fujita's aircraft grew steadily worse. He managed to

**Lt Zenji Abe saw considerable action in Type 99s at Pearl Harbor, in the Indian Ocean and the Aleutians (*Zenji Abe*)**

maintain formation for a while, but as fuel dwindled, the kanbaku inevitably slowed and lost altitude. Fujita waved a handkerchief as the aeroplane headed down. Then, when the undercarriage hit the water, both he and his observer, WO Mitsuo Cho, perished as the dive-bomber flipped over on its back and quickly sank out of sight.

Having observed many ships still in harbour and continued opposition by flak and enemy fighters, Cdr Fuchida radioed the task force at 0828 hrs requesting preparation of a second attack. Kido Butai's floatplanes had been out searching for the British fleet since early morning but had reported nothing so far. Thus, at 0852 hrs, Nagumo ordered his reserve force of Type 97s aboard *Zuikaku* and *Shokaku* to replace their torpedoes with bombs for a second strike on Colombo. A third of the Type 99s on the other carriers also exchanged their ordinary bombs for land bombs.

Aeroplanes from the initial strike began arriving back aboard the carriers at 0948 hrs. For the loss of five Type 99s from *Zuikaku* and one from *Shokaku*, as well as a single Zero-sen from *Soryu*, the airmen of Kido Butai had downed six Swordfish, 21 Hurricanes and four Fulmars. Most had fallen to the Zero-sens, but dive-bomber crews also claimed a few.

At 1000 hrs, while the strike force was still being recovered, a Type 94 Mk 2 Reconnaissance Seaplane (Kawanishi E7K2) from the heavy cruiser *Tone* radioed a contact report following the sighting of what appeared to be two enemy cruisers 150 miles west of the task force. Nagumo immediately launched additional floatplanes to follow up the contact, and at 1023 hrs he ordered the 5th Koku Sentai Type 97s to attack these ships with torpedoes. Chaos ensued on the hangar decks of *Zuikaku* and *Shokaku* as the ordnance crews, who had been in the process of re-arming the aeroplanes with bombs, now frantically reversed course and began arming them with torpedoes once more.

At 1050 hrs, however, a Type 94 Mk 2 Reconnaissance Seaplane from the light cruiser *Abukuma* mistakenly reported the enemy vessels as destroyers. At 1127 hrs, therefore, Nagumo ordered just the dive-bombers of the reserve force to take off. In response, 53 Type 99s winged their way toward the enemy ships, the pressure to launch quickly having left 16 of them still armed with 242 kg land bombs from the first re-arming order. With Lt Chihaya in the sick bay, his subordinate, Lt Zenji Abe, led 17 off the fleet flagship *Akagi* at 1149 hrs. Eighteen kanbaku from *Hiryu*, led as usual by Michio Kobayashi, followed ten minutes later, while *Soryu* launched 18 shortly thereafter, led by Takashige Egusa. As senior officer, Egusa took command of the entire force.

Meanwhile, one of the follow-up search aeroplanes – a Type 0 Reconnaissance Seaplane (Aichi E13A1) from *Tone*, spotted the ships at 1155 hrs and correctly reported them as *Kent* class cruisers, with no other vessels visible for 20 miles. They were the heavy cruisers *Cornwall* and *Dorsetshire*, racing to join Somerville's fleet to the southwest, having cleared Colombo harbour the night before. IJN doctrine maintained that heavy cruisers, like battleships, could only be sunk by air attack if torpedoes were used. At 1310 hrs, therefore, Nagumo ordered the Type 97s launched once again, their take-off now scheduled for 1400 hrs.

Lt Cdr Egusa had by then radioed his sighting of the ships, spotting the vessels as early as 1254 hrs. They were in quarter formation, with *Dorsetshire* leading to starboard. The dive-bombers approached from astern, hidden

The heavy cruisers *Cornwall* (left) and *Dorsetshire* (right) twist and turn in vain as bombs dropped by 52 Type 99s find their mark on 5 April 1942. Both vessels were sunk in record time thanks to perfect conditions for dive-bombing – the cruisers were attacked from dead ahead and down sun, which created a blind spot for the ships' anti-aircraft gunners. Literally every bomb dropped either struck the vessels or scored a telling near miss (*wwiiarchives.net*)

from view by a thick cloud bank between themselves and their quarry. At 1329 hrs Egusa ordered the commencement of 'Attack Method No 2. Bomb heading 50 degrees. Wind 230 degrees, six metres'.

Attack Method No 2 in IJN dive-bomber jargon entailed an echelon left formation, with the leader on the right closest to the target and the attack being executed by shotai. Attack Method No 1 involved a long, line astern formation of the entire chutai, with each aircraft diving in sequence. This allowed greater accuracy, but also exposed each aircraft to greater risk, and was increasingly used only against lightly defended targets as the war progressed. Attack Method No 3 was an echelon right.

With a light breeze behind them from the southwest, the kanbaku dived out of the sun in a northeasterly direction, bow-on to the ships, commencing the actual attack at 1338 hrs. Egusa ordered *Hiryu's* trailing formation to attack the nearer lead ship, *Dorsetshire*, while he led *Soryu's* aircraft against the more distant second vessel, *Cornwall*. Attacking *Dorsetshire*, Kobayashi's bomb penetrated the quarterdeck and disabled the steering. His two wingmen also scored, wrecking the wireless stations and knocking out most of the vessel's anti-aircraft guns on its port side.

Against *Cornwall*, Egusa achieved a near miss to port abreast the bridge, which caused flooding in the port bulges and wrecked the port low power room, causing the steering motors to fail after the rudder had been put hard-a-starboard. His No 2, FPO 2/c Takeo Yamazaki, scored a direct hit between the forward and centre funnel, while the third bomb near-missed to starboard abreast the hangar, penetrated the hull beneath the waterline and killed everyone in the aft engine room. Thereafter, both ships were pummelled by a devastating succession of hits and near misses.

The dive-bombers from *Akagi* now followed, starting their attack at 1345 hrs. Abe split his force, sending Shohei Yamada's second chutai of eight against *Dorsetshire*, while he himself went after *Cornwall* with his first chutai of nine. One bomb hung up on its rack and was not released, but most of the others found their mark. The attack ended at 1355 hrs, a mere 17 minutes after it had begun.

The Type 99 Carrier Bomber crews of 1st and 2nd Koku Sentai had this day achieved one of the highest hit ratios ever recorded in combat against freely manoeuvring warships at sea in the history of dive-bombing. Having absorbed ten reported hits and several near misses, *Dorsetshire* capsized to port and sank stern first at 1348 hrs, just ten minutes from the start of the attack. After suffering nine hits and six near misses, *Cornwall* followed ten minutes later, also on her port side, down slightly by the bows. Egusa immediately reported both ships sunk.

Surprised by the speed and seeming ease with which the two warships had been destroyed, *Akagi* flashed a signal to 5th Koku Sentai just in time to prevent the torpedo-laden Type 97s from taking off. At 1405 hrs, *Tone's* Type 0 Reconnaissance Seaplane reported seeing no enemy after searching 50 miles along the cruisers' original track to the southwest, and the attack aeroplanes stood down. Had this floatplane continued on for just ten or fifteen miles more, it would have spotted Somerville's Force 'A', which by this time was only 84 miles from where the cruisers had been sunk. Instead, the floatplane turned back, fuel running low. All dive-bombers had returned without loss by 1445 hrs.

Somerville still hoped to engage Nagumo in a night action, and he had closed to within 150 miles of Kido Butai by late afternoon, probing to his northeast. Two scouting Albacores from *Indomitable* actually sighted Nagumo's fleet, but Zero-sens from *Hiryu* intercepted both, shooting one down before it could send a message and driving off the other before it could send a full report. A confusing signal received later that day sent Somerville to the northwest. But Nagumo was withdrawing southeast, and the two forces drew apart during the night. Somerville continued to search for the Japanese fleet over the next two days, but finally retired to Addu on the 8th. Here, in conference with his senior commanders, he realised just how outmatched he was, prompting him to send Force 'B' to Mombasa, in East Africa, while he led Force 'A' to Bombay. The British Eastern Fleet would not return to Ceylon until September 1943.

Kido Butai had continued to withdraw eastward during 6 April so as to get beyond search range of British aircraft, before swinging north and closing on the naval base at Trincomalee, on the northeast coast of Ceylon, on the 8th. The task force was spotted by a Catalina that day and its transmission duly intercepted, but it was decided to carry out a raid as planned. At 0600 hrs on 9 April Nagumo's carriers launched 91 attack aircraft and 38 fighters against Trincomalee, but held back all the dive-bombers in case any elements of the British fleet turned up.

At 0755 hrs a Type 95 Reconnaissance Seaplane (Nakajima E8N2) from the battleship *Haruna* reported 'Enemy carrier *Hermes* and three destroyers 250 degrees, 155 miles from starting point'. In response to this signal, 85 Type 99s and nine Zero-sens were sortied from 0843 hrs – 17 dive-bombers from *Akagi*, 18 each from *Soryu*, *Hiryu* and *Shokaku* and 14 from *Zuikaku*, plus three Zero-sens each from *Soryu*, *Hiryu* and *Akagi*, all under the overall command of *Shokaku's* Kakuichi Takahashi.

The vessels were heading south, having cleared Trincomalee harbour in anticipation of the IJN raid. With the attack having ended at 0745 hrs, they had turned back north. *Hermes* carried only two damaged Swordfish under repair in its hangar, the rest having been left ashore at China Bay, Trincomalee, when the vessel sailed. The ships had no air cover.

Takahashi arrived at the carrier's anticipated position off Ceylon's southeast coast at 0950 hrs, but finding nothing, he led his dive-bombers south along the target's reported track for some 40 miles without success. He finally found *Hermes* off Batticaloa Lighthouse after reversing course and flying north for some 30 minutes, reporting his sighting at 1030 hrs.

Takahashi ordered the attack five minutes later and dropped the first bomb at 1040 hrs, scoring a hit on the carrier's flightdeck. He was followed in quick succession by the two wingmen of his command shotai, the nine aeroplanes of Lt Yamaguchi's 1st chutai and the six-aircraft 2nd chutai, now led by Lt(jg) Shozo Koizumi after the loss of Lt Fujita on the 5th.

*Shokaku's* dive-bombers claimed 13 hits out of 18, demolishing the flightdeck and blowing the forward lift completely out of its well. Five minutes later *Zuikaku's* Type 99s, led by Akira Sakamoto, attacked, his 1st chutai of six and Tamotsu Ema's 2nd chutai of eight claiming 13 hits out of 14. They were followed by Kobayashi's aeroplanes from *Hiryu*.

When the British heavy cruisers had been attacked four days earlier, the partial use of land bombs with instantaneous fuses had proven very effective in suppressing the ships' anti-aircraft fire. Now against *Hermes*, six of *Hiryu's* dive-bombers were deliberately armed with 242 kg land bombs for just this purpose, while the rest carried 250 kg ordinaries. By the time 11 of *Hiryu's* Type 99s had completed their dives on *Hermes*, claiming nine hits, the carrier was clearly doomed, down by the bow and listing heavily to port with its flightdeck awash. Nonetheless, Lt Zenji Abe, leading *Akagi's* contingent, and his wingman, FPO 1/c Tamotsu Akimoto, added two more hits to speed *Hermes* on its way to the bottom.

In yet another textbook demonstration of their prowess, the Type 99s of Kido Butai had destroyed an aircraft carrier in the space of 15 minutes, claiming 37 hits out of 45 bombs dropped. British reports estimated hits by 'at least 40 bombs, the remainder being very near misses'.

Seeing that *Hermes* was clearly finished, Lt Michiji Yamashita (*Hiryu's* 2nd chutai leader) and three others from his chutai promptly switched their attention to the carrier's escort, the Australian destroyer HMAS *Vampire*, as did 12 of the dive-bombers from *Akagi*. A concentration of hits and damaging near misses tore the destroyer in half, its destruction culminating in an explosion of the after magazine shortly before the vessel sank at 1105 hrs, and an underwater explosion two minutes later.

But a shotai each from *Hiryu* and *Akagi* did not join in. These six aeroplanes went after the 5868-ton tanker *British Sergeant* some 12 miles northwestward instead, achieving four direct hits and two near misses. The tanker's buoyancy prevented it from sinking immediately, the vessel eventually foundering off Elephant Point, 17 miles north of Batticaloa, two hours after first being attacked at 1100 hrs.

The 18 dive-bombers from *Soryu* were the last on the scene. Robbed of the glory of participating in the destruction of *Hermes*, Takashige Egusa, on his own initiative, led his formation further north in response to a report of a second carrier in that direction from *Abukuma's* scout, whose navigation would prove no better than its ship identification skills. After flying north for more than 20 miles without sighting the alleged carrier, Egusa gave up the search and turned back south, resigned to attacking less attractive targets passed up earlier. Time expended in this detour would spell tragedy for *Soryu's* Type 99s.

Meanwhile, Kakuichi Takahashi assembled *Shokaku's* dive-bombers starting at 1105 hrs and withdrew

HMS *Hermes* became the first aircraft carrier to be sunk by carrier-based dive-bombers on 9 April 1942. Devoid of fighter cover, the vessel quickly succumbed to multiple direct hits from the Type 99s that had sortied from *Shokaku, Zuikaku, Hiryu* and *Akagi* (*Fleet Air Arm Museum*)

from the battle area, followed by aeroplanes from *Zuikaku*, *Hiryu* and *Akagi*. The Zero-sen escort went with them, nobody having noticed *Soryu's* Type 99s heading northward. Egusa's formation was on its own.

En route back to Kido Butai, *Shokaku's* dive-bombers and three fighters from *Hiryu* came upon five Blenheim IV bombers of No 11 Sqn RAF who were returning home following an attack on Nagumo's ships.

No 11 Sqn had been searching for the IJN carriers almost daily since the attack on Colombo. They finally found their quarry on 9 April and made their attack at 1048 hrs, just as the dive-bombers were pounding *Hermes*. Eleven Blenheim IVs had taken off from Colombo's Racecourse at 0820 hrs, but two had aborted with engine trouble, leaving nine in the actual attack. Lookouts aboard Kido Butai had failed to spot their approach, and the first inkling of an attack had come only when water spouts straddled *Akagi* and also erupted near the cruiser *Tone*. The bombs missed and no damage was done, but Nagumo's task force had been attacked for the first time since the start of the war. *Akagi* failed to fire a single shot in its own defence, so sudden and unexpected was the assault.

Defending Zero-sens had then pursued the Blenheim IVs as they withdrew, shooting down four in return for the loss of *Hiryu's* fighter buntai leader, Lt Sumio Nono, to return fire from the bombers. The Blenheim IVs suffered further at the hands of Takahashi's returning formation between 1135 hrs and 1147 hrs, losing the aeroplane of Sqn Ldr Ken Ault to *Hiryu's* escorting Zero-sens and *Shokaku's* Type 99s, although they managed again to down one of the Zero-sens in return.

At 1200 hrs Egusa's dive-bombers from *Soryu*, having wasted over an hour in their fruitless detour to the north, found the corvette HMS *Hollyhock* escorting the 5571-ton auxiliary fleet oiler *Athelstane* some 30 miles south-southeast of Batticaloa. They also spotted the 2924-ton Norwegian freighter *Norviken*. *Soryu's* 18 kanbaku split up, six attacking *Athelstane* at 1205 hrs and quickly sinking it with several hits, while six others began bombing *Hollyhock* three minutes later, putting it under at 1218 hrs. The remaining six went after *Norviken*, leaving the ship badly damaged and adrift, eventually to break up and sink the following evening after running aground.

Toward the end of these attacks, at 1215 hrs, and shortly after one kanbaku had departed early with engine trouble, the bombers, in turn, were attacked by six Fulmars of No 273 Sqn RAF and eight Fulmars from 803 and 806 NASs. These aircraft had finally arrived on the scene after responding to a distress call from *Hermes*. In a running battle lasting 25 minutes, four *Soryu* Type 99s went down and four others were damaged. In return, the kanbaku managed to destroy two Fulmars. Egusa himself claimed one, expending 200 rounds from his forward guns.

Kido Butai began recovering aeroplanes from *Zuikaku*, *Hiryu* and *Akagi* at 1245 hrs, Takahashi arriving 20 minutes later with the *Shokaku* bombers and two remaining *Hiryu* fighters, delayed by their encounter with the Blenheim IVs. Egusa returned 20 minutes after Takahashi at 1325 hrs with 13 Type 99s from *Soryu*. His 2nd shotai leader, Lt Moriyuki Koide, crashed his battle-damaged aircraft on the flightdeck.

So ended Kido Butai's foray into the Indian Ocean. Although it had failed in its objective of destroying the British Eastern Fleet, it had forced the latter's withdrawal to the western Indian Ocean. The Royal Navy

Acknowledged throughout the IJN as being its finest dive-bomber leader, Lt Cdr Takashige Egusa led the Type 99s of the second wave during the attack on Pearl Harbor, and also presided over the sinking of the British cruisers *Cornwall* and *Dorsetshire* in the Indian Ocean in April 1942. Ultimately, he fell in battle on 15 June 1944 leading Ginga (P1Y1) land-based bombers of 521 Ku in action against US carriers in the Marianas *(Michael Wenger)*

would not pose a direct threat to Japan's Greater East Asian Empire for two full years. Above all, in the destruction of *Cornwall*, *Dorsetshire* and *Hermes*, the 'Hell Divers', as the men of the IJN's kanbaku corps liked to style themselves (dive-bomber crews of the IJN were particularly fond of the 1931 Hollywood film *Hell Divers*, and adopted this American moniker for themselves), had demonstrated unequalled prowess and awesome destructive power.

The chance discovery that land bombs worked well in suppressing shipboard anti-aircraft fire was a pleasant surprise, leading *Hiryu's* Detailed Action Report to recommend that the first shotai of each dive-bomber chutai be so armed for attacks on heavy cruisers and carriers.

But there were also some critical lessons to be learned from Operation *C*. That enemy bombers had attacked the task force without warning was highly disturbing. Both *Hiryu's* report, as well as a comprehensive paper on battle lessons prepared by Yokosuka Kokutai, urged installation of radar on Japanese carriers at the earliest opportunity. 5th Koku Sentai's Detailed Action Report emphasized the need to improve air search capabilities, pointing out that sightings from scout aeroplanes had a direct bearing on command decisions. Yokosuka Kokutai's report also recommended greater training in ship recognition, and the stationing of six to nine examples of the new 13-Shi Carrier Bomber (Yokosuka D4Y), then under development as a successor to the Type 99, as high-speed scouts aboard each carrier division flagship. Significantly, in retrospect, these recommendations all emphasized speed and accuracy of ship identification, rather than thoroughness of search. No voices called for two-phase search patterns.

Confusion and delay caused by bewildering changes in arming orders experienced on 5 April resulted in a training exercise aboard *Hiryu* in order to gain precise data on the amount of time required by ordnance crews to make such changes. But none of these concerns could dampen the triumphant mood within Kido Butai. The officers and men of Nagumo's fleet now held a growing conviction that wherever they sailed, victory would surely follow.

Kido Butai retired eastward and passed through Malacca Strait on 13 April. Next day, due east of Singapore, 5th Koku Sentai received two Zero-sens, four Type 99s and one attack aeroplane from *Akagi*, plus eight Zero-sens and six Type 99s from 2nd Koku Sentai, while giving up three Zero-sens and two Type 99s to *Akagi* and two Zero-sens to *Soryu*. 5th Koku Sentai then split off from Nagumo's fleet and headed for Mako (Makung), Taiwan, to replenish in preparation for its next operation, which would take it to Truk and onward into the Coral Sea. Akira Sakamoto now departed *Zuikaku*, having been transferred to Yokosuka Kokutai. Tamotsu Ema became *Zuikaku's* new kanbaku leader.

Then, on the morning of 18 April, came shocking news of the Doolittle raid on Japan. Nagumo's carriers, then passing through Bashi Channel between Luzon and Taiwan, immediately changed course and went charging eastward in an effort to intercept the carriers. However, it was soon realised that the enemy had withdrawn after unleashing Doolittle's B-25s against the Empire. The sacred soil of Dai-Nippon had been violated by an audacious enemy. Adm Yamamoto was mortified.

Something had to be done about these US carriers once and for all.

# CORAL SEA – THE CARRIERS CLASH

With first stage operations having achieved the conquest of Southeast Asia, Combined Fleet officially launched second stage operations on 10 April 1942. For Vice Adm Inoue's South Seas Force, a major objective of the second stage was Operation *MO* – the capture of Port Moresby on the south coast of Papua New Guinea and Tulagi in the Solomon Islands. *MO* was originally scheduled for April with just the fleet carrier *Kaga*, but American carrier activity had upset Japanese plans yet again.

On 10 March, during Japanese landings at Lae and Salamaua on New Guinea's north coast, ships of the invasion force lying offshore had endured a series of raids by Allied aircraft, including 104 US Navy aeroplanes from the carriers *Lexington* and *Yorktown*, resulting in four ships being sunk and nine others damaged. *MO* was postponed until May, as losses had to be made good and repairs effected before the operation could take place. With memories of 10 March still fresh, *Kaga* was replaced by *Zuikaku* and *Shokaku* in Combined Fleet's final second stage operations order of 10 April.

The operational plan for *MO* devised by 4th Fleet staff was a complex affair involving five separate formations, including the Tulagi Invasion Force, *MO* Force Main Body, a Support Force to establish seaplane bases in the region and the Port Moresby Invasion Force. The strongest element of the entire operation would be Rear Adm Chuichi Hara's 5th Koku Sentai, to be teamed with an escort provided by Rear Adm Takeo Takagi's 5th Sentai (heavy cruisers *Myoko* and *Haguro*) and two destroyer divisions, to form *MO* Mobile Force. Under the rigid seniority protocols of the IJN, Takagi (soon to be promoted to vice admiral on 1 May) had overall command of Mobile Force, but by mutual consent Hara remained in charge of air operations, subject to consultation with Takagi. Hara reached Truk on 25 April from Mako while Takagi arrived from Yokosuka with his cruisers two days later.

By April 1942 Adm Chester W Nimitz, Commander-in-Chief, Pacific Fleet enjoyed a priceless advantage over his rival Yamamoto thanks to the quality of his radio intelligence. While the latter had reacted futilely, after the fact, to a series of hit-and-run raids by his enemy's surviving carriers, Nimitz was now able to anticipate the IJN's moves and deploy his precious post-Pearl Harbor assets accordingly. By mid-April, US naval intelligence could say with confidence that Japan's next move would come in the Coral Sea at month-end. This would threaten the entire Allied strategic position in the South Pacific and could not be ignored.

Rear Adm Aubrey Fitch's Task Force 11, with the carrier *Lexington*, sailed from Pearl Harbor on 15 April and headed south. It would join

Rear Adm Frank 'Jack' Fletcher's *Yorktown* task force (TF-17) already in the South Pacific. On 25 April Vice Adm William Halsey returned to Pearl Harbor from Doolittle's Tokyo raid with *Enterprise* and *Hornet* (TF-16). It was doubtful that Halsey's carriers could steam 3500 miles to the Coral Sea in time to see action, but after five days of furious preparation they left Pearl Harbor in an attempt to do so nonetheless.

*MO* Main Body, with the light carrier *Shoho*, departed Truk on 30 April. Mobile Force, with the big fleet carriers *Zuikaku* and *Shokaku*, followed Main Body out of Truk on 1 May, but encountered bad weather before the day was out. By late afternoon the task force could no longer recover returning patrol aeroplanes safely. These were forced to head back toward Truk. A dive-bomber and an attack aeroplane from *Zuikaku* crash-landed on Lossop Island, while another attack aeroplane managed to reach Truk but could not rejoin Mobile Force as it continued heading south so as to stay on schedule.

In addition to their own aircraft complements, *Zuikaku* and *Shokaku* carried nine extra Zero-sens between them to be ferried to Rabaul prior to the main operation – a seemingly simple task. However, a storm front northeast of New Ireland would frustrate this mission, forcing the carriers to remain in that area on both 2 and 3 May, upsetting their schedule.

On 4 May, the day after Japanese troops went ashore at Tulagi, the invasion force there was attacked by a succession of raids by SBDs, TBDs and F4Fs. Clearly, at least one American carrier lurked somewhere in the Coral Sea, but Mobile Force was badly out of position and unable to strike back. Having wasted two full days on the abortive ferrying attempt, it was still some 340 miles northwest of Tulagi, and had just begun refuelling when news came of the attack. Refuelling was cut short and the carriers sped southeast, but it soon became clear that they were beyond striking range.

Adm Inoue, who had advanced to Rabaul from Truk on 4 May to direct the overall course of Operation *MO*, decided confidently that the Americans would be dealt with in due course by Mobile Force, and kept *MO* to schedule. The Port Moresby Invasion Force sailed from Rabaul that same day. It was scheduled to transit Jomard Passage in the Louisiade Archipelago during the evening of the 7th, with the Port Moresby landing set for the pre-dawn hours of 10 May. Meanwhile, Mobile Force continued southeast along the northern fringe of the Solomons. It reached the eastern end of the archipelago at midday on 5 May, then rounded San Cristobal and entered the Coral Sea from the east.

Fletcher, who had rendezvoused briefly with Fitch on 1 May, now rejoined him south of Guadalcanal on the morning of the 5th and began refuelling from the fleet oiler *Neosho*. *Yorktown's* fuel consumption of the previous two days in raiding Tulagi had been heavy. He resumed refuelling on the 6th, sailing further northwest overnight to close the distance on the invasion force expected to come through Jomard Passage.

The morning of the 6th also found Takagi's Mobile Force engaged in refuelling operations, so rudely interrupted by Fletcher's Tulagi raid on the 4th. As Takagi's cruisers took on fuel from the fleet oiler *Toho Maru* south of New Georgia, Japanese air search efforts drew a bead on Fletcher. A Type 97 Flying Boat (Kawanishi H6K) of Yokohama Ku out of Tulagi radioed a morning contact and confirmed the existence of a carrier in the enemy formation. However, navigational error placed the Americans some 50 miles south of their actual position. Believing the enemy vessels to be further south than they actually were, Hara concluded that he would be unable to get within striking distance that afternoon. Takagi decided to complete refuelling first and prepare to give battle on the 7th.

Meanwhile, Fletcher had cut short his refuelling and had resumed his northwesterly course, detaching *Neosho* and the destroyer USS *Sims* (DD-409) to the south. Although neither side realised it, the opposing forces converged and were only 70 miles apart at one point that evening. The Japanese had missed a golden opportunity earlier that day to catch Fletcher while he refuelled, but there was conviction on both sides that the following day would bring action.

On the night of 6 May Hara counted 109 aircraft operational out of 121 aboard his two carriers – 19 of 20 Zero-sens, 17 of 22 Type 99 Bombers and 17 of 21 Type 97 Attack Aeroplanes on *Zuikaku*, and all 18 Zero-sens, 19 of 21 Type 99s and all 19 Type 97s on *Shokaku*.

At 0600 hrs on 7 May, *Zuikaku* and *Shokaku* each launched six Type 97 Attack Aeroplanes to search for the American task force. Hara directed them to the southwestern quadrant, from 180 to 270 degrees, out some 250 miles, mindful of the previous day's flying boat contact. In an effort to improve air search capabilities following the Indian Ocean experience, 5th Koku Sentai had been sending search aeroplanes out in pairs since the start of Operation *MO*, although still adhering to single-stage search patterns. Unfortunately, the two crews from *Shokaku* assigned to the southernmost 180-degree sector were among the least experienced. Their inept observations would cause deep trouble for Hara.

Fifteen minutes after Hara launched his Type 97s, Fletcher despatched ten SBDs from *Yorktown* to cover an arc northwest to northeast from 325 to 085 degrees, again out 250 miles, in the direction of Bougainville. Misleading radio intelligence had placed the main Japanese carrier force in that area. Fletcher had no idea that it was actually in his rear to the east. At 0625 hrs, TF-17 reached a point 170 miles southeast of Deboyne and turned northward, detaching Australian Rear Adm John G Crace with two heavy cruisers, a light cruiser and three destroyers to proceed directly to Jomard Passage. This left Fletcher with *Yorktown* and *Lexington*, four heavy cruisers and eight destroyers.

At 0722 hrs, one of the two *Shokaku* scouts flying the 180-degree search sector radioed that they had spotted an enemy force at 182 degrees, 163 miles from base, and added at 0745 hrs that it included 'one aircraft carrier'. This was precisely what Hara had been waiting for. Between 0800 hrs and 0815 hrs, Hara launched nine Zero-sens, 17 Type 99 Bombers and 11 torpedo-armed Type 97 Attack Aeroplanes from *Zuikaku* and nine Zero-sens, 19 Type 99s and 13 torpedo-armed Type 97s from *Shokaku*. Kakuichi Takahashi led the dive-bombers, and he was also in overall command. Although he had received notice of promotion to 5th Koku Sentai air staff officer, effective 1 May, Takahashi had volunteered to continue in his role as *Shokaku* hikotaicho until the end of *MO*. *Zuikaku* hikotaicho Shigekazu Shimazaki, led the Type 97s.

At 0815 hrs, as Takahashi assembled his formation over Mobile Force and headed south, Fletcher received a report from one of his SBD scouts, pinpointing a Japanese fleet, including 'two carriers', 225 miles northwest of his position at the northern entrance to Jomard Passage. As with Hara earlier, this was the news Fletcher had been waiting for. The American carriers closed range over the next hour and *Lexington* launched 19 F4Fs, 28 SBDs and 12 TBDs starting at 0926 hrs. With no doctrine of integrating their air groups as the Japanese did routinely, *Yorktown* followed with eight F4Fs, 25 SBDs and ten TBDs in a strike of its own 18 minutes later.

Early morning of 7 May found the Port Moresby Invasion Force 25 miles north of Deboyne, headed for Jomard Passage, while the cruisers of *MO* Main Body and the light carrier *Shoho* trailed 25 miles behind to the north-northeast. Main Body had been discovered by Flying Fortresses flying from Australia at 0748 hrs and was subsequently bombed without effect.

Meanwhile, Main Body's cruiser floatplanes were also busy scouring the Coral Sea. At 0820 hrs, a mere five minutes after Mobile Force had sent off its air strike to the south, a Type 94 Mk 2 Reconnaissance Seaplane from the heavy cruiser *Furutaka* reported what appeared to be an enemy task force 150 miles southeast of Deboyne, west of Mobile Force. This was followed ten minutes later by a report from the heavy cruiser *Kinugasa's* Type 94 Mk 2 identifying several warships, including a carrier, in the same general area.

It seemed that the Americans were in two or more separate groups. But Hara had already launched a maximum effort strike to the south. His confident message to that effect to all forces at 0900 hrs was disturbing news for Main Body and the Invasion Force, which had assumed that Hara's aeroplanes would attack the enemy reported by the cruiser floatplanes. Those ships remained free to attack the Invasion Force. The transport convoy was ordered forthwith to reverse course and retire northward until the danger had passed.

Hara's confidence waned as the minutes ticked by. Strangely, no reports came from his strike force. What Takahashi's aeroplanes spotted at 0912 hrs turned out to be an oiler and a destroyer, the *Neosho* and *Sims*. Takahashi and Shimazaki searched for the supposed carrier for almost two hours but found nothing.

Meanwhile, *Yorktown* had recovered its SBD scouts by 1024 hrs, only to discover that the earlier contact report of two carriers had actually been for cruisers, this signal being sent incorrectly due to a misaligned coding device. Fortunately for Fletcher, a report of the early morning B-17 contact, which definitely included one carrier positioned some 30 miles south of the SBD contact, had finally reached *Yorktown* at 1022 hrs. At 1053 hrs Fletcher transmitted in the clear, redirecting the American strike groups toward this new target.

Two minutes earlier, at 1051 hrs, bad news had reached *Zuikaku's* bridge. The 180-degree sector scouts, finally realising their error, had radioed that their initial report of a carrier had been in error, as they had actually spotted the oiler *Neosho*. Chagrined, Hara immediately recalled his strike. At 1115 hrs, Takahashi ordered Shimazaki back to Mobile Force, while he attempted to turn this mess into something positive. He led several of *Shokaku's* Type 99s against the destroyer *Sims*, sinking the vessel in a matter of minutes with three direct hits – one of these caused a boiler to explode, tearing the ship in two as it sank. Only 15 sailors from a crew of 250 survived.

The rest of *Shokaku's* dive-bombers, followed by all 17 from *Zuikaku*, concentrated on *Neosho*, scoring seven hits and eight near misses. The ordinary bombs, with 0.2-second delayed-action fuses, punctured the thin deck plating of the oiler, causing massive destruction below decks, but gave the appearance from above of having little effect. American anti-aircraft fire proved formidable as always. A *Zuikaku* Type 99 piloted by FPO 2/c Shigeo Ishizuka erupted in flames, but the crew held its dive and released its bomb. In a supreme effort, just as his aeroplane was about to hit the sea, Ishizuka pulled the nose up and slammed into the side of *Neosho's* No 4 gun, turning the oiler's deck into a raging inferno. Gutted and listing 30 degrees to starboard, *Neosho* drifted until 11 May, when it was scuttled by the destroyer USS *Henley* (DD-391).

Witnessing the first genuine jibaku (self-destruct) from among their ranks in this war, the self-sacrifice of Ishizuka and his observer, FPO 3/c Masayoshi Kawagoe, made a deep impression on all of *Zuikaku's* dive-bomber crews.

At 1110 hrs, shortly before Takahashi had commenced his attack on *Neosho* and *Sims*, the Americans had targeted the light carrier *Shoho*, devastating the flattop with 13 bomb and seven torpedo hits that caused the vessel to sink at 1135 hrs.

Takahashi assembled *Shokaku's* dive-bombers and withdrew at 1205 hrs, returning to his carrier an hour later. *Zuikaku's* Type 99s departed the scene later and had trouble finding their way back, the last of them not touching down until 1515 hrs. Meanwhile, in a final display of their ineptitude, the two *Shokaku* 180-degree scouts became lost during their return and ended up crash-landing on Indispensable Reef to the east.

Throughout the day, various Japanese search aeroplanes had made contact both with Fletcher's carriers and Crace's Support Force further west. Having wasted a maximum effort strike against *Neosho* and *Sims*, however, Hara could do nothing until his aircraft were recovered. Moreover, updated position reports seemed to place the enemy carriers beyond the range of Mobile Force. Shortly after 1500 hrs, however,

This is the last known photograph taken of the *Neosho*. It was snapped by a Japanese aeroplane at noon on 7 May 1942, Type 99 bombers having attacked both the oiler and its escort, the destroyer *Sims*. Despite a 30-degree list, the ship would continue to float for four days until the surviving 123 crewmen were rescued by the destroyer USS *Henley* (DD-391) on 11 May (*US Naval Historical Center*)

Already on fire, *Neosho* vainly attempts to out-manoeuvre upwards of 30 Type 99s (*US Naval Historical Center*)

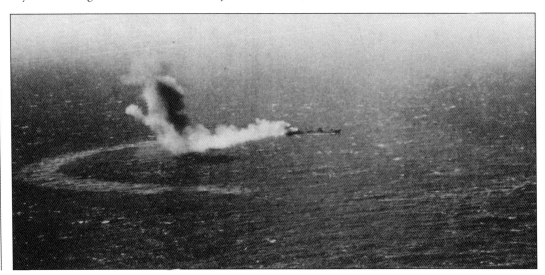

A fine view of *Shoho* on 20 December 1941. Note the lack of an island. Navigation was accomplished from a small bridge located under the forward part of the flightdeck. This vessel was sunk on 7 May 1942 during the Battle of the Coral Sea (*Yamato Museum*)

a report originally sent at 1407 hrs by a Type 94 Mk 2 from the heavy cruiser *Aoba* brought unexpected news that the enemy fleet had changed course to the southeast. Quick calculations showed that if the enemy maintained this course and speed, he would come within striking range of 5th Koku Sentai by 1830 hrs. That was a long shot. It would also be 15 minutes after sunset, requiring a night landing. But now under great pressure, with *Shoho* already lost to the Americans, Hara felt compelled to take the risk. Only the most experienced and night qualified aircrews were chosen for the mission.

At 1615 hrs Kakuichi Takahashi led six dive-bombers and six attack aeroplanes from *Shokaku* and six dive-bombers and nine attack aeroplanes from *Zuikaku* westward, with orders to fly a heading of 277 degrees out some 280 miles. By his calculations Takahashi did not expect to join battle for more than two hours. With action anticipated after sunset, there was no fighter escort. An earlier navigational error by *Aoba*'s scout was now about to cause tragedy.

By 1600 hrs, Fletcher's carriers were actually only 190 miles west of Mobile Force. At around 1745 hrs the Japanese passed some 30 miles south of TF-17 in heavy overcast, quite unaware of their quarry nearby. US radar picked up the IJN aircraft, however, and F4Fs from VF-2 and VF-42 were vectored out to intercept. Without warning, shortly before 1803 hrs, the torpedo-laden Type 97s at the rear of the Japanese formation were ambushed by F4Fs. Five *Zuikaku* and two *Shokaku* Type 97s burst into flames and fell to the Grummans in quick succession. The crew of one damaged *Shokaku* Type 97 heroically attempted to return home, but ditched short of the carrier and perished. The Type 99s up ahead, knowing they would be next, tightened formation and braced for the onslaught, but after only a brief exchange of fire the F4Fs departed, recalled by their fighter director officer aboard *Lexington* as fuel ran low.

Torpedoes now jettisoned, the surviving attack aeroplanes straggled back toward Mobile Force. With his dive-bomber formation still intact, Takahashi continued to search doggedly for the American carriers in the gathering gloom, but finally abandoned his efforts at 1820 hrs. The kanbaku now shed their bombs and began their return flight, unaware that TF-17 lurked only 20 or 30 miles to the east, between themselves and Mobile Force. After about 30 minutes the kanbaku crews spotted the welcome silhouettes of two carriers engaged in recovering aircraft. In their tense and exhausted state, the men were all too eager to assume that Adm Hara had sped forward to shorten the length of their return flight.

Faint light on the western horizon was fading fast as the dive-bombers flew into the twilight zone and approached the ships. 'Entering landing course', Takahashi announced to his observer, Res Ens Hoei Nozu, and switched on his approach lights and running lights. However, not seeing the carrier's familiar landing aid lights, Takahashi had Nozu flash a signal with an Aldis lamp, asking 'Are we cleared for landing?' In contrast to American and British carriers, in which aeroplanes were guided in using manual visual signals by a landing signal officer (LSO) on the flightdeck, IJN carriers employed a system of lights that allowed the pilots to guide themselves in without the need for an LSO.

The responding flashes from *Lexington* looked like the Japanese signal for 'OK'. Takahashi rocked his wings, giving the order to break formation and enter the landing pattern. Seeing this, Ema and the *Zuikaku* aeroplanes also prepared to land on 'their' carrier to starboard. Down below, personnel aboard the carriers realised that there were too many aeroplanes in the landing pattern. Some of these aircraft had strange elliptical wings, yet one of the mystery aeroplanes had flashed a signal that looked like the American 'F' code for friendly aircraft, sowing confusion. On both sides something had been lost in translation.

As Ema came in on what he thought was *Zuikaku*, his observer, WO Fujikazu Azuma, gave a shout as he recognised the alien profile of a tripod mast on one of the escorting cruisers. Ema later recalled, 'I flew past without landing and leaned out of my cockpit. Things just didn't look right. Then, just as it dawned on me that this might be the enemy, all hell broke loose'.

It was 1909 hrs, and *Yorktown* doused its deck lights and opened fire. Fire also came from surrounding ships and an F4F in the air. The kanbaku scattered like agitated wasps. Hit by flak, Ema's No 2 (WO Susumu Koyama/observer-commander, and FPO 1/c Toshio Inagaki/pilot) fell in flames as the sole dive-bomber loss of the mission. The rest eventually straggled back to their own carriers, guided by homing signals and by Mobile Force assuming a special formation for recovery of aircraft at night, taking the supreme risk of illuminating the fleet despite the enemy's proximity.

In the end, *Zuikaku* recovered five dive-bombers and four attack aeroplanes, while *Shokaku* recovered all six dive-bombers, but only three of its attack aircraft. Returning crews cursed their bad luck in having discarded their ordnance before stumbling upon the American carriers in a close encounter of the most dubious kind. For the Japanese, so far in this battle nothing had gone right.

At 2040 hrs Adm Inoue ordered the Port Moresby landings postponed for two days, and the heavy cruisers *Kinugasa* and *Furutaka* detached from Main Body to beef up Mobile Force. Both carrier forces now realised that the other was close by – they were less than 100 miles apart. To avoid undue convergence during the night, Takagi led Mobile Force due north at 2210 hrs immediately after recovering aircraft, while Fletcher steamed southeast.

By 2230 hrs, Hara had 96 aircraft ready for the fight the next day – 19 fighters, 14 bombers and 12 attack aeroplanes aboard *Zuikaku*, and 18 fighters, 19 bombers and 14 attack aeroplanes aboard *Shokaku*. Fletcher would have 117 operational next morning – 14 fighters, 32 dive-bombers and nine torpedo-bombers aboard *Yorktown*, and 17 fighters, 33 dive-bombers and 12 torpedo-bombers aboard *Lexington*.

With his attack aeroplane strength greatly depleted and no prospect of relying on cruiser floatplanes for the next morning's search because of attrition and heavy seas, Takagi, at Hara's suggestion, decided after midnight to begin the morning air search from a position 120 miles further north. This would allow a narrow search pattern focused southward with only a few aeroplanes, instead of 360-degree coverage.

On 8 May, between 0615 hrs and 0625 hrs, three *Zuikaku* and four *Shokaku* attack aeroplanes took off and split up as they searched an arc 140 to 230 degrees out to a distance of 250 miles. Each aircraft flew alone, Mobile Force no longer having the luxury of flying paired searches. In contrast to the previous day, all aeroplanes were manned by experienced crews. On the American side, *Lexington* launched 18 SBDs in a 360-degree search starting at 0625 hrs.

The belt of low pressure across the Coral Sea that had helped to cloak TF-17 in previous days had drifted northward. Together with the relative movements of the opposing forces, this now exposed Fletcher under clear skies, while squally weather aided the Japanese. At 0822 hrs a *Shokaku* scout flying the 200-degree search sector transmitted, 'Enemy carrier force sighted'. There followed a succession of detailed and accurate reports from the seasoned aircraft commander/observer, WO Kenzo Kanno, leaving no doubt that this was indeed the main enemy task force.

Between 0910 hrs and 0915 hrs, nine Zero-sens, 14 Type 99s and eight Type 97s took off from *Zuikaku*, while *Shokaku* launched nine

**The US carrier task force TF-17 as photographed by a Japanese reconnaissance aircraft just prior to it being attacked. The large ship in the centre is *Lexington* (*Edward M Young*)**

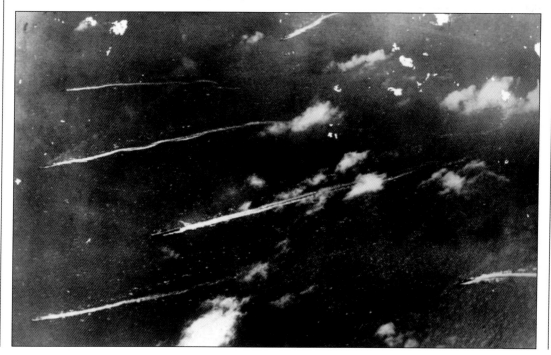

Zero-sens, 19 Type 99s and ten Type 97s. Indefatigable Kakuichi Takahashi once again led the total strike force of 69 aircraft southward on a heading of 196 degrees, with the carriers chasing after them at 30 knots in an effort to shorten their return flight.

Meanwhile, an SBD scout from *Lexington's* VS-2 had spotted Mobile Force and had sent a contact report at 0820 hrs, prompting TF-17 to launch a strike of its own against the Japanese carriers – *Yorktown* despatched six F4Fs, 24 SBDs and nine TBDs, while *Lexington* sent nine F4Fs, 15 SBDs and 12 TBDs. Widely separated according to doctrine, both American strike groups were on their way by 0925 hrs. One *Lexington* TBD aborted with engine trouble.

At 1045 hrs, as it proceeded at an altitude of 3000 m, the Japanese strike force came upon Kanno's returning Type 97. In an act of supreme courage, with full knowledge that remaining fuel would not guarantee a safe return, Kanno's crew reversed course and guided Takahashi's strike unerringly toward the enemy. Apparently a later victim of US fighters, Kanno's aeroplane did not make it back.

At 1105 hrs the American task force came into view to the southwest beneath clear skies flecked with scattered clouds and haze at lower altitudes. With Takahashi's order of 'To tsu re' ('deploy attack formation'), the kanbaku began their climb to 5000 m while the torpedo-bombers went down to 1200 m. Approaching from the northeast, the attack order 'To, To, To, To' went out at 1110 hrs. A minute later, with *Lexington* leading and *Yorktown* trailing to the southwest, the American carriers turned to starboard onto a heading of 125 degrees, placing the oncoming Japanese on their port beams.

Takahashi took his 33 dive-bombers on a wide clockwise circle to the southeast in order to attack from upwind, while Shimazaki led the torpedo-bombers straight for the carriers. The *Shokaku* Type 97s circled right to approach *Lexington's* port bow, while half of *Zuikaku's* eight banked left and attacked it to starboard, leaving four *Zuikaku* machines charging *Yorktown's* port beam. The heavy loss of Type 97s the previous evening had left too few for a full 'anvil' attack on both carriers.

**'EI-208' from *Shokaku* over TF-17, minutes before the main battle on 8 May 1942 (*Shigeru Nohara*)**

Despite 20 minutes' radar warning, the American CAP was badly deployed and failed to block the Japanese attack. Indeed, only one *Zuikaku* torpedo-bomber was shot down prior to the actual assault on the carriers. Seven more (two from *Zuikaku* and five from *Shokaku*) fell to fighters and flak during their torpedo runs and the withdrawal. *Yorktown* successfully combed all torpedoes aimed at it, but two torpedoes from *Shokaku*'s Type 97s slammed into *Lexington*'s port side. These hits jammed the forward flightdeck elevator, buckled the port aviation gasoline tanks and flooded several compartments, forcing three boilers to be shut down. *Lexington* fought on with a 6.5-degree list to port and speed reduced to 24 knots.

At 1121 hrs, in near perfect coordination, almost simultaneously with the second torpedo hit came Takahashi's 19 kanbaku from *Shokaku*. His command shotai of three was followed by Lt Masao Yamaguchi's 1st chutai of nine and Lt Iwakichi Mifuku's 2nd chutai of seven. They were now deployed in single file, having arrived over *Lexington* without interference from the American CAP. With the big flattop in view 30 degrees to their right as it continued its starboard circle, and a ten-metre wind out of the southeast, the Type 99s pushed over into the teeth of *Lexington*'s anti-aircraft fire.

One of the first bombs dropped struck the portside forward 5-in gun gallery and detonated in the ready ammunition locker, killing gun crews and starting a fire in the admiral's cabin. Having completed its starboard turn, the big carrier now steamed westward, forcing the kanbaku into shallower crosswind dives, throwing off their aim. They did, however, score upwards of five near misses, some very close aboard, wrecking a 20 mm gun emplacement, opening several underwater seams and flooding two compartments. A second bomb struck the port side of the huge smoke stack, jamming the ship's siren and killing men at the 0.50-cal machine gun mounts on both sides of the stack.

As the last trio of *Shokaku* dive-bombers made their attack, American fighters finally appeared. An F4F-3 from VF-42 flown by Lt(jg) Arthur J Brassfield shot down shotai leader WO Hidenori Matsuda (FPO 1/c Takeo Nobe/observer), prompting his two wingmen to abort their dives and switch to *Yorktown*. They became the last aeroplanes to attack the latter vessel, but the No 3 (FPO 3/c Akishige Kaku/pilot and F 1/c Noboru Matsuda/observer) fell to Lt Albert O Vorse Jr of VF-2.

Having to fly farther to reach *Yorktown*, which was southwest of *Lexington*, Lt Tamotsu Ema's 14 kanbaku from *Zuikaku* had pushed over at 1125 hrs – several minutes after the torpedo attack on that carrier had ended. With *Yorktown*'s helm able to give undivided attention to the assault from above, the *Zuikaku* bombers smothered Fletcher's carrier with a dozen near misses, but registered

*Lexington* under attack from Type 99 dive-bombers on 8 May. Of the 19 *Shokaku* dive-bombers that attacked the ship, two scored direct hits, while five others scored near misses. One of the dive-bombers can be seen above *Lexington* to the right moments after it had completed its attack (*US Naval Historical Center*)

only one hit. At 1127 hrs, a No 25 Ordinary Bomb hit the flightdeck squarely amidships, penetrated three decks and exploded just above the armoured fourth deck. It wiped out a repair party, caused significant structural damage and knocked out the air search radar. Shrapnel damage shut down three boilers, reducing speed to 25 knots. The ship now also trailed oil, one of the near misses to port having opened fuel tanks to the sea.

Two of *Zuikaku's* Type 99s succumbed to anti-aircraft fire from the ship. In Ema's lead chutai, the aeroplane of shotaicho Lt Takashi Kuzuhara (FPO 1/c Koji Kawase/observer) suddenly belched black smoke while in the dive. Engulfed in flames, it plunged into the sea just ahead of *Yorktown's* bow. FPO 2/c Isao Kamioka (F 1/c Kiyoshi Izumi/observer) from Lt Reijiro Otsuka's second chutai also failed to make it through.

Following their dives, the kanbaku headed for their post-strike rendezvous 30 miles north of the target. Following their assault on *Yorktown*, the *Zuikaku* bombers turned left. Tamotsu Ema briefly exchanged shots with an SBD, but otherwise the *Zuikaku* bombers encountered no enemy aircraft in the vicinity and withdrew without further loss. *Shokaku's* Type 99s were not so lucky. Turning right after attacking *Lexington*, they found their way barred by several F4Fs and SBDs. Both *Shokaku* chutai leaders, Lts Yamaguchi and Mifuku, saw Takahashi's command shotai up ahead battling enemy aeroplanes at low altitude and rushed to help. In the ensuing dogfight, Mifuku was seriously wounded in his right eye during a head-on pass with an F4F. It was also the last that anyone saw of Lt Cdr Kakuichi Takahashi.

Yamaguchi reached the rendezvous point and was joined there by Mifuku and three *Shokaku* Zero-sens. They formed up with Ema and one *Zuikaku* Zero-sen that was already there, but Lt Cdr Takahashi never turned up. The highly respected and senior-most kanbaku leader on active carrier duty and his observer, Ens Nozu, were probably killed in the dogfight. Four other *Shokaku* dive-bombers failed to return for a total of seven lost, along with their crews, from that carrier. One was claimed to Lt(jg) William N Leonard of VF-42 returning to TF-17 as part of *Yorktown's* strike on Mobile Force, while two others fell to Lt Noel Gaylor of VF-2 in the returning *Lexington* strike.

A somewhat indistinct, but compelling, photograph of *Lexington* as seen from one of the attacking Japanese aircraft. The carrier is already burning, and the number of splashes around the ship suggests that this shot was taken during the dive-bombing attack (*US Naval Historical Center*)

*Yorktown* suffered only a single direct bomb hit during the battle. Here, sailors clear away debris from the third deck compartment that the bomb exploded in. Despite appearances, the damage was relatively light and the ship remained operational (*US Naval Historical Center*)

Ema, Yamaguchi and Mifuku also encountered returning US strike aircraft but managed to get away as Zero-sens in their formation confronted the Americans.

The Japanese attack on TF-17 had ended by 1140 hrs. Despite the damage inflicted, both US carriers appeared to be in good shape, and flight operations remained unimpaired. *Lexington's* list was promptly corrected and its fires nearly extinguished. *Yorktown* also brought matters quickly under control. Then, at 1247 hrs, a huge explosion shook *Lexington*. Deep in the bowels of the ship, sparks from untended electric motors had touched off fuel vapours leaking from the ruptured port gasoline stowage tanks. The resulting fires spread out of control, triggering a series of violent explosions that ultimately doomed the ship.

As the survivors of the Japanese strike force returned to Mobile Force, they saw that *Shokaku* was badly hurt, billowing ominous black smoke from the bow and with its flightdeck buckled. Between 1057 hrs and 1150 hrs, the American strike groups had scored three 1000-lb bomb hits on it at the cost of six SBDs, one TBD and four F4Fs shot down or subsequently ditched.

At 1230 hrs, unable to recover aircraft, *Shokaku* directed its aeroplanes to *Zuikaku*, which was unscathed, having been hidden inside a rain squall when the attack began. But not all aeroplanes got the word. A Type 99 and a Zero-sen ignored wave offs and managed to land aboard *Shokaku*, despite non-functioning arresting wires.

Between 1310 hrs and 1430 hrs, *Zuikaku* recovered 44 aircraft, including ten of its kanbaku, plus seven more from *Shokaku*. Eleven damaged aircraft from both carriers ditched. *Zuikaku's* torpedo leader, Shigekazu Shimazaki, came down near the destroyer *Shiratsuyu*. One *Zuikaku* dive-bomber crash-landed on Tagula Island, the crew later being recovered by the seaplane carrier *Kamikawa Maru*. A *Zuikaku* CAP Zero-sen came down at Deboyne. The heavy cruiser *Furutaka* rescued three other *Shokaku* fighter pilots from the CAP, two *Shokaku* Type 99 crews and a Type 99 crew from *Zuikaku*. Later, the repair ship *Shoei Maru* rescued another *Shokaku* dive-bomber crew, and one more dive-bomber from the carrier apparently ditched too, but the details of the crews' rescue remain unclear.

Not knowing how many aeroplanes from both carriers there were to recover, *Zuikaku's* deck crew aggressively discarded aircraft overboard – some with only minor damage. In all, six *Zuikaku* and six *Shokaku* aeroplanes went over the side (three fighters, four bombers and five attack aeroplanes). These included Lt Mifuku's Type 99, shot full of holes, but also Lt Ema's 'EII-235', his trusty mount since Pearl Harbor, which was undamaged apart from a nearly severed left aileron joint.

Returning strike leaders were certain they had sunk the *Saratoga*-class carrier, but were unsure about *Yorktown*. Lt Ema reported only serious damage to the second carrier, but command decided to report both carriers sunk. Later that afternoon, Mobile Force counted 24 Zero-sens, nine Type 99s and six Type 97s operational. An additional Zero-sen, eight Type 99s and four Type 97s could be made ready following repair. But Hara decided that a second strike was out of the question. Takagi radioed 'no prospect of a second strike today' at 1430 hr and withdrew Mobile Force to the north to take stock of his remaining strength and refuel his ships. Wounded *Shokaku* had already been headed north under escort since 1220 hrs.

Fletcher was in no better shape. By 1300 hrs *Yorktown* had recovered five F4Fs, 21 SBDs and nine TBDs from its strike group. Of the vessel's total complement, only seven F4Fs, 11 SBDs and eight TBDs were fit for immediate duty. In light of his enemy's superiority in fighters and possession of an undamaged carrier, Fletcher retired southward at 1324 hrs. By 1413 hrs, despite continued internal explosions and fires, *Lexington* recovered a total of five F4Fs, 12 SBDs and ten TBDs from its strike. At 1422 hrs, however, Fitch transmitted a disturbing, though mistaken, report that a third large Japanese carrier may have joined the fight, prompting complete withdrawal by Fletcher. *Lexington* remained stubbornly afloat into the evening but finally slid beneath the waves at 1952 hrs after being torpedoed by the destroyer USS *Phelps* (DD-360).

Adm Nimitz concurred with Fletcher's decision to withdraw. His radio intelligence reported growing indications that the Japanese were up to something big in the central Pacific, and he would need all his carriers back at Pearl Harbor to meet the challenge.

On the Japanese side, Adm Inoue decided to cancel the entire operation. At 1545 hrs he ordered Mobile Force to cease the attack and retire northward, and called for an indefinite postponement of Operation *MO* at 1620 hrs. Combined Fleet was irate over Inoue's apparent lack of aggressiveness. Not yet aware of the extent of aeroplane losses, Yamamoto countermanded Inoue at 2200 hrs and ordered him to pursue and destroy remaining enemy forces. Mobile Force dutifully reversed course and headed south at high speed after refuelling on the 9th. By then the moment had passed, however. Its scout aeroplanes finding only *Neosho*, derelict and adrift, *Zuikaku* headed north again at 1230 hrs on 10 May.

The Battle of the Coral Sea, history's first naval action fought entirely by aircraft in which opposing surface forces never came within sight of each other, was finally over.

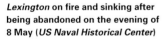

***Lexington*** **on fire and sinking after being abandoned on the evening of 8 May (*US Naval Historical Center*)**

# MIDWAY AND THE ALEUTIANS

Midway was a vexed operation from the start. The Japanese high command realised the importance of seeking a swift end to the war before the full impact of American industrial might was felt on the battlefield. Yet by early March 1942, with the planned launch of second stage operations only a month away, there was still no consensus on how ultimate victory was to be achieved. Naval General Staff and Combined Fleet were at loggerheads once again.

Naval General Staff had championed an operation to capture New Caledonia, Fiji and Samoa in order to cut the supply line from the USA to Australia. However, with alternate island routes in the region, Yamamoto had doubts that such an operation would succeed. Instead, he proposed to capture Midway Atoll on Hawaii's doorstep. That, surely, would bring America's remnant fleet out to fight. For Yamamoto, final destruction of the US Pacific Fleet was the key to victory. America's surviving carriers had to be crushed.

The resulting compromise, tentatively reached on 5 April 1942, set a blistering pace for conquest. Following the capture of Port Moresby in May, Midway was to be seized in June. Landings on New Caledonia, Fiji and Samoa would take place during July. Then, if all went well, Combined Fleet aspired to invade Hawaii sometime around October. As part of the quid pro quo with Naval General Staff, Combined Fleet also agreed to undertake an operation against the Aleutian Islands in the far north.

All opposition to Yamamoto's proposal evaporated with the Doolittle raid of 18 April. Those who had earlier opposed the Midway plan were now forced to see the value of capturing a patrol base close to Hawaii. Moon and tide considerations dictated that 7 June would be the ideal date for the Midway landing. Both Midway (Operation *MI*) and the Aleutians (Operation *AL*) were planned as a single, integrated undertaking.

Kido Butai returned to Japan from the Indian Ocean on 22 April. With the scheduled departure for Operation *MI* barely one month away, there was no time to lose – ship repair and replenishment schedules proved nearly impossible to meet. Rear Adm Yamaguchi would transfer his flag to *Hiryu* on 8 May when repairs to *Soryu* appeared to be delayed. Time for

*Ryujo* **was the IJN's first light carrier. It had embarked the IJN's first operational dive-bomber unit in 1933, but for the Aleutians operation of June 1942 only Zero-sens and Type 97 attack aeroplanes flew from its flightdeck. The vessel operated alongside** *Junyo* **during Operation** *AL* **(***Kure Maritime Museum***)**

training replacement aircrew was appallingly short, especially as personnel transfers to provide cadre for new units caused widespread disruption. Lt Zenji Abe, junior dive-bomber buntai leader on *Akagi*, now became senior dive-bomber leader aboard the new carrier *Junyo*. Among veteran kanbaku pilots reporting to him was Shinsaku Yamakawa from *Kaga*, recently promoted to flight petty officer 3rd class.

The 27,500-ton *Junyo*, converted from the NYK liner *Kashiwara Maru*, was commissioned on 3 May and assigned to 4th Koku Sentai, joining the old carrier *Ryujo*, which had returned to Kure Naval Base on 23 April from a successful sortie in the Bay of Bengal. Together, they formed the nucleus of Rear Adm Kakuji Kakuta's 2nd Kido Butai, assigned to the Aleutians operation. Nagumo's task force, destined for Midway, now became 1st Kido Butai.

The Battle of the Coral Sea on 8 May was hailed as a victory by the IJN, despite the subsequent failure to capture Port Moresby. Aircrew losses and damage to *Shokaku* would prevent both it and *Zuikaku* from participating in the upcoming operation. This did not overly concern Combined Fleet, who felt confident that the four carriers of 1st and 2nd Koku Sentai, the elite of Nagumo's task force, were more than a match for anything the Americans could throw at them. Oblivious to US Navy breakthroughs in cryptanalysis, IJN preparations for Midway proceeded on the widely held and fundamentally flawed belief that surprise would be achieved, and that enemy carriers, if they chose to appear at all, would do so only in reaction after the landings had been completed.

For Operation *AL*, *Ryujo* carried 12 Zero-sens (plus four spares) and 18 Type 97 Attack Aircraft (plus two spares), while *Junyo's* air group counted six Zero-sens (plus two spares) and 15 Type 99 Bombers (plus four spares). Additionally, on 19 May, *Junyo* embarked 12 Zero-sens of the newly formed 6th Ku to be delivered to Midway following the conclusion of Operation *AL*. A further 21 Zero-sens of 6th Ku were taken aboard carriers of Nagumo's 1st Kido Butai on the 23rd – six onboard *Akagi*, nine on *Kaga* and three each on *Hiryu* and *Soryu*.

During a final round of war-games and meetings held on 25 May, 1st Kido Butai announced that it could not sail on schedule because of delays in the delivery of aircraft spare parts, resulting in a one day delay in departure and a consequent one day delay in launching air attacks on Midway. Unaffected by Nagumo's delay, Kakuta's 2nd Kido Butai departed Ominato, in northern Honshu, as scheduled on 26 May. The early hours of 3 June across the International Date Line found the task force 180 miles southwest of their target – Dutch Harbor on the Aleutian island of Unalaska. Starting at 0325 hrs, *Junyo* launched 13 Zero-sens and 15 Type 99 Bombers, while *Ryujo* launched six Zero-sens (three aborted) and 14 Type 97 Attack Aeroplanes.

With cloud ceiling down to 300 m, the two carrier air groups flew separately. Zenji Abe led his dive-bombers at an altitude of just 200 m, wondering whether the overcast would abate sufficiently for them to gain height and dive-bomb. He decided it would not and aborted the mission, much to the displeasure of Rear Adm Kakuta. *Ryujo's* horizontal bombers managed to get through. Finding clear weather over Dutch Harbor, with a cloud ceiling over 3000 m, its aeroplanes attacked the radio station, tank farm, barracks at Fort Mears and moored PBYs. During the withdrawal, they spotted five destroyers in Makushin Bay, southwest of Dutch Harbor, and had a brief brush with P-40s, without loss.

Kakuta now decided to go after the destroyers. He launched four Type 95 Reconnaissance Seaplanes to search ahead, then sent out his second strike of the day from 1045 hrs – nine Zero-sens and 17 Type 97s from *Ryujo* and six Zero-sens and 15 Type 99s from *Junyo*. This time foul weather and freezing carburettors forced all aeroplanes to abort except for two floatplanes from the heavy cruiser *Takao*. These were intercepted by P-40s, one being shot down and the other, badly damaged, abandoned after crew recovery.

Unsatisfied with results thus far, Kakuta was determined to raid Dutch Harbor again the next day. Zenji Abe was under great pressure. Knowing that another abort would not be tolerated, regardless of the weather, he decided to take only seasoned crews, dropping the inexperienced third wingmen from each shotai and reducing the size of his strike to 11 bombers. Meanwhile, the foul weather hampered American air efforts as well. None of the B-17s and B-26s sent to attack Kakuta's carriers during 4 June scored any hits. Encounters with P-40s indicated an airfield near Dutch Harbor, but the Japanese had no idea where.

Starting at 1640 hrs on 4 June, *Ryujo* launched six Zero-sens and nine Type 97s, while *Junyo* sent five Zero-sens and Abe's 11 Type 99s. They eventually managed to penetrate the heavy cloud cover and reached brilliant sunshine above 2000 m. Luckily, a solitary opening in the clouds lay just above Dutch Harbor, and Zenji Abe (WO Shoro Ishii/observer) led them through. Just before the attack, however, one dive-bomber and Lt Yoshio Shiga, leader of the *Junyo* fighter escort and overall leader of the *Junyo* strike, were forced to turn back with engine trouble. Starting at 1810 hrs, attacking from the south in shallow dives due to surrounding clouds, the Type 99s set fire to the barracks ship *Northwestern*, demolished part of a hospital and bombed oil tanks, anti-aircraft artillery positions and the naval air station hangar and pier.

Following the attack, Abe turned west toward the narrow passage between Unalaska and Umnak Island, heading for the main assembly point above the southwestern tip of Unalaska. He was followed by his third shotai leader, FPO 1/c Kazutoshi Numata (FPO 2/c Yoshio Takano/observer) and WO Nobuo Harano (FPO 1/c Ichiro Nakajima/observer), a shotaicho from the second chutai. Low clouds kept them at an altitude of 200 m. As fate would have it, the chosen assembly point turned out to be directly across from the USAAF airfield at Otter Point, on Umnak. What Abe thought were friendly Zero-sens up ahead turned out to be eight P-40Es of the 11th FS.

Concerned that suddenly seeking cloud cover would invite a mid-air collision, Abe decided to fight it out, trusting to the Type 99's superior manoeuvrability. During this desperate fight, he caught a glimpse of Otter Point airfield. Then realising that he was now alone, he ducked into cloud. Harano and Numata had fallen to the P-40s. Abe flew on, his aircraft peppered with ten bullet holes, including one 50 cm wide in his right wing. The aeroplane of Abe's second shotai leader, WO Hiroshi Yamamoto (FPO 1/c Sachio Oishi/pilot) had been badly hit by flak over the harbour and was eventually forced to ditch. A destroyer was sent to the rescue, but Yamamoto and Oishi were never seen again.

Shortly after Abe's encounter with the P-40s, Lt Naohiko Miura (FPO 1/c Hiroyasu Kawabata/pilot), second chutai leader, reached the assembly point along with Shinsaku Yamakawa (now paired with FPO 2/c Tsuyoshi Nishiyama, who was observer/commander) and FPO 2/c Takeshi Sugie (FPO 3/c Tadao Okada pilot). As Yamakawa flew along at an altitude of 300 m, munching contentedly on a rice ball, tracer fire suddenly zipped past his right wing. He snapped his head back to find a gaggle of Warhawks closing on his 'six o'clock', with Sugie and Okada nowhere in sight. Yamakawa side-slipped his aircraft as Nishiyama in the rear seat fired his hand-held 7.7 mm machine gun for dear life. The Warhawks bored in, their fire kicking up spray on the ocean surface as Yamakawa lost altitude in desperate evasive manoeuvres.

Then, just when all seemed lost, *Junyo's* WO Saburo Kitahata and FPO 1/c Yukiharu Ozeki of 6th Ku – both Zero-sen aces – came up behind them and drove off the P-40s, probably shooting down 2Lt John J Cape Jr. Meanwhile, Sugie and Okada had engaged a P-40 (possibly that of 2Lt Winfield E McIntyre) in a separate action, claiming it shot down with Okada's forward guns, before heading back to *Junyo.*

With his hydraulics shot out, Zenji Abe could not deploy his flaps. Landing without them, he used up most of the flightdeck and nearly fell overboard before catching the last wire forward of the bridge and nosing over. By the time Shinsaku Yamakawa had returned, with his two Zero-sen saviours in tow, the thickening fog had reduced visibility to under a mile. The carrier loomed up like a ghost, with landing aid lights glowing dimly through the murk, but they managed safe landings. Sugie and Okada never made it. Alone, they struggled through the darkening mist, asking for bearings. Their radio, however, damaged in the fight, could transmit but not receive. Their squadron mates on *Junyo* heard the drone of an engine nearby, but it grew faint as the aeroplane flew away. In the end, Sugie rapped out 'No fuel left. We will self-destruct. Long live the Emperor!' and disappeared into the night.

*Junyo* had lost four dive-bombers and their crews. The *Ryujo* strike returned with the loss of one Zero-sen. A month later, the US Navy would find this virtually undamaged aeroplane flipped over in the tundra on Akutan Island east of Dutch Harbor, and duly unlock the secrets of Japan's fearsome Zero-sen fighter.

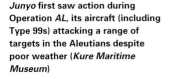

*Junyo* first saw action during Operation *AL,* its aircraft (including Type 99s) attacking a range of targets in the Aleutians despite poor weather (*Kure Maritime Museum*)

Before launching the 4 June strike, Adm Kakuta had received shocking news of mayhem at Midway and orders from Combined Fleet (originally transmitted at 1420 hrs) to head south with all due speed and join forces with Nagumo. However, judging that three days would be needed to comply, Kakuta had decided to launch his Dutch Harbor strike first. After terminating aeroplane recovery at 2026 hrs, he dutifully headed south, but Combined Fleet's order was later cancelled, and Kakuta remained in northern waters.

Off duty personnel aboard IJN ships often loitered near the radio room in the hope of catching interesting news, but the transmissions from Midway were appalling. 'Enemy disinformation' declared some, 'No, it's true' whispered others. *Junyo's* radio room was now declared off-limits to all but essential personnel. The following week, a vessel from Destroyer Division 4 hove to and transferred airmen from *Soryu* by boat. Aboard *Junyo* came a pitiful lot – many barefooted, others with no caps, some with no shirts. Shinsaku Yamakawa recognised his pilot trainee classmate and fellow kanbaku aviator FPO 3/c Motomu Kato among them. 'Hey, what happened?' shouted Yamakawa, as his classmate shuffled past. 'We got hit' was Kato's curt reply. The men from *Soryu* were quickly segregated, and for the next three days all communication with them was forbidden. Scuttlebutt coursed through the decks. Something terrible must have happened at Midway.

## DISASTER AT MIDWAY

With preparations finally completed, Nagumo's 1st Kido Butai had weighed anchor and sortied from Hashirajima anchorage on 27 May. As Nagumo's carriers got underway, Bill Halsey's TF-16, with *Enterprise* and *Hornet*, entered Pearl Harbor, where it was still 26 May. Fletcher's TF-17 with the damaged *Yorktown* arrived the next day. With clear knowledge of Japanese intentions, a sense of crisis gripped the Pacific Fleet. In a Herculean round-the-clock effort, minimum emergency repairs needed to make *Yorktown* seaworthy and battle-ready were completed in just three days. TF-16, now commanded by Rear Adm Raymond A Spruance, left Pearl on 28 May, while Fletcher's TF-17 following two days later.

Although 1st Kido Butai was in the vanguard, Operation *MI* involved most of Combined Fleet, organised into a number of separate formations, including the Main Force under Adm Yamamoto himself in his flagship *Yamato*. These forces were too widely dispersed for mutual support, however. Ultimately, only 1st Kido Butai would play a key role in the forthcoming battle.

Japanese efforts to acquire advanced warning of US carrier movements all came to naught. An operation to send four-engined Type 2 Flying Boats (Kawanishi H8K1s) over Pearl Harbor had to be cancelled on 31 May when submarines found French Frigate Shoals – the designated refuelling stop for the flying boats – occupied by American surface vessels. Submarine picket lines were positioned roughly halfway between Oahu and Midway athwart the likely route of American carrier deployment from Pearl Harbor. But by the time the submarines, dogged by delays, arrived on station, the US carrier task forces had already traversed these lines and passed to the northwest.

Spruance and Fletcher rendezvoused northeast of Midway during the afternoon of 2 June. Fletcher, the senior commander, directed TF-16 to remain ten miles to his south, then advanced both task forces westward overnight to a position 260 miles north of Midway.

A PBY from Midway spotted ships of the Japanese invasion convoy southwest of the atoll on the morning of 3 June, and a night torpedo attack by PBYs in the early hours of the 4th damaged the oiler *Akebono Maru*. On the Japanese side, Main Force intercepted a radio message in the predawn hours indicating possible enemy carrier activity north of Midway. Mindful of maintaining radio silence, however, Yamamoto's staff declined to relay this news to Nagumo, assuming that he, 300 miles closer to Midway, would have also monitored this signal. He had not. 1st Kido Butai closed on Midway from the northwest, blithely unaware that American carriers already lay in wait.

Chronology for the Battle of Midway is particularly complex as it was literally fought across the International Dateline. In the interest of simplicity, all subsequent time references in this chapter are given according to Midway Local Time, east of the Dateline.

Nagumo's carriers counted 247 aircraft operational, including the 6th Ku Zero-sens. *Akagi's* own air echelon possessed 18 Type 0 Fighters, 18 Type 99 Bombers and 18 Type 97 Attack Aircraft. *Kaga's* had 18 fighters, 18 bombers and 27 attack aeroplanes, plus two extra bombers apparently transferred from *Soryu*. *Hiryu's* own air echelon counted 18 each of the three types, while *Soryu's* had 18 fighters and 18 attack aeroplanes, but only 16 kanbaku, as it had apparently transferred two to *Kaga*. In place of this pair, in partial fulfillment of recommendations following Indian Ocean operations, *Soryu* carried two of the latest D4Y1 bombers (designated Type 2 Carrier Reconnaissance Aircraft) as high-speed scouts. One was damaged in a landing mishap shortly after departing Hashirajima, however, leaving only one operational. In addition, each ship carried a trio of partially dismantled Zero-sens, Type 99s and Type 97s as spares.

Arrayed against them were 225 aircraft aboard the American carriers (27 F4F-4s, 37 SBD-2/3s and 14 TBD-1s aboard *Enterprise*, 27 F4F-4s, 34 SBD-3s and 15 TBD-1s aboard *Hornet* and 25 F4F-4s, 34 SBD-3s and 12 TBD-1s aboard *Yorktown*), plus a total of 127 aircraft of various types on Midway itself. Far from bringing overwhelming air power to the battle, Nagumo's airmen were outnumbered. However, these were the IJN's elite, the world's finest naval aviators of their day.

Starting at 0430 hrs on 4 June, 1st Kido Butai launched 108 aircraft against Midway, 210 miles to the southeast – 18 bomb-carrying Type 97 Attack Aeroplanes each from *Hiryu* and *Soryu*, and 18 Type 99 Bombers each from *Akagi* and *Kaga*, all escorted by 36 Zero-sens (nine from each carrier). Engine trouble forced one *Hiryu* attack aeroplane to abort after take-off. With *Akagi's* Mitsuo Fuchida still recovering from an appendectomy, the overall strike was commanded by *Hiryu* hikotaicho Lt Joichi Tomonaga, who was piloting the carrier's lead Type 97. Lt Shoichi Ogawa from *Kaga* led the kanbaku force.

Together with the launch of the Midway strike, 1st Kido Butai despatched seven aircraft in a widely spaced and porous search along the eastern semi-circle – five cruiser floatplanes north of Midway and two carrier attack aeroplanes south of the atoll. Except for the northernmost line, which was to be flown by the battleship *Haruna's* short-ranged Type 95 Reconnaissance Seaplane, all were to fly out 300 miles and then turn left for 60 miles before heading back. The cruiser search seaplanes faced various delays. The heavy cruiser *Tone's* Type 0 Reconnaissance Seaplane 'No 4', in particular, which had been assigned to the 100 degree line, was held up by catapult trouble and, unbeknownst to Nagumo, did not take off until 0500 hrs.

Combined Fleet had given strict orders for half of 1st Kido Butai's air strength to be held in readiness to attack the enemy fleet in case it appeared – 43 torpedo-armed Type 97s (17 from *Akagi* and 26 from *Kaga*) and 34 Type 99s (18 from *Hiryu* and 16 from *Soryu*), together with 24 Zero-sens (six from each carrier), stood by for this task. But at 0520 hrs Nagumo announced his intent to direct this reserve force against Midway if the situation remained unchanged. Aboard the carriers, land bombs were brought up to the hangar decks in anticipation of a possible ordnance change.

At 0532 hrs ships at the front of Nagumo's formation began laying smoke after their lookouts spied an enemy flying boat – Nagumo's ships still lacked radar. At 0534 hrs and 0552 hrs, two separate PBYs from Midway each sent contact reports of two Japanese carriers. These transmissions were also picked up by the American carriers. Midway's own aeroplanes were scrambled after its radar picked up Tomonaga's incoming strike shortly before 0600 hrs. Seven minutes later Fletcher ordered Spruance to 'proceed southwesterly and attack enemy carriers as soon as definitely located', the report of only two carriers having left open the possibility of more in the area.

Having taken just 15 minutes to assemble, the Japanese strike force had moved out at 0445 hrs with Zero-sens from *Akagi* and *Kaga* sweeping ahead, while those from *Hiryu* and *Soryu* positioned themselves above and behind the bombers and attack aeroplanes as direct escorts. Midway Atoll, with its two small islands, Sand and Eastern, came into view at 0615 hrs and Tomonaga gave the order to deploy for attack two minutes later. The Type 97 Attack Aeroplanes surged forward, ready to initiate the assault, while the Type 99 Bombers began their climb to 4000 m. The forward fighters, meanwhile, were now out of position, distracted by a false 'bandit' sighting and leaving their charges dangerously exposed. It was at that moment that real enemy fighters struck.

US Marine Corps fighters of VMF-221 managed one clean pass, concentrating on the attack aeroplanes, downing two from *Hiryu* and damaging several others, including puncturing the right main wing tank on Tomonaga's lead machine. Then the Zero-sens arrived. In short order, 13 F2A-3s and two F4F-3s were shot down and their pilots killed. The Zero-sens suffered just two damaged in the fight.

Starting at 0634 hrs, and now free from interference from enemy fighters, Tomonaga's attack aeroplanes bombed the atoll's two islands with 800 kg land bombs. One *Hiryu* Type 97 fell to flak over Eastern Island, while two others (one each from *Hiryu* and *Soryu*) damaged earlier by enemy fighters eventually ditched with the loss of both crews.

With the attack aeroplanes having completed their bombing runs, the Type 99s from *Akagi* and *Kaga* went to work with their 242 kg land

Lt Joichi Tomonaga was commander of *Hiryu's* air group at Midway. Flying a Type 97, he played an important part in the battle as the commander of the Japanese strike on Midway atoll on the morning of 4 June and later as the commander of the second strike on *Yorktown,* which ultimately led to the destruction of the American carrier (*US Naval Historical Center*)

bombs from 0640 hrs. *Akagi's* dive-bombers hit the airfield and other facilities on Eastern, suffering two aeroplanes damaged, while those from *Kaga* struck Sand Island, hitting the seaplane hangar, officers' quarters, barracks and oil tanks there. One *Kaga* dive-bomber fell to flak over Sand, while four others received damage. The Zero-sens came down to strafe but lost two, one to flak and one to an enemy fighter.

At 0700 hrs Tomonaga sent a pre-arranged signal indicating that a second strike on Midway was needed. Now, a series of key decisions and events over the next two hours would decide the ultimate course of battle.

0700 hrs was also about the time that 1st Kido Butai's search aeroplanes would have reached the end of their outward leg, assuming

Midway Atoll is composed of two islands. Eastern Island in the foreground contained the airfield and Sand Island, across the channel, was home to a seaplane base. Midway was the lure used by Yamamoto to force the Pacific Fleet to confront the assembled might of Combined Fleet (*US Naval Historical Center*)

that they were on schedule. Nagumo waited 15 minutes following Tomonaga's message, but with no word from his search aeroplanes, at 0715 hrs, he ordered the ordnance change to prepare his reserve force for a second strike on Midway. Loading land bombs on the kanbaku was relatively easy, but exchanging torpedoes for land bombs on the attack aeroplanes involved the replacement of attachment racks. This was a laborious process that could easily consume more than two hours even under ideal conditions.

Influencing Nagumo in his decision had been the arrival at 0710 hrs of the first attacks from Midway in the form of six TBF-1s of VT-8's land-based detachment, which were making the aeroplane's combat debut, and four USAAF B-26s armed with torpedoes. Five TBFs and two B-26s fell to the defending Zero-sens in exchange for two IJN fighters downed by the bombers' return fire. No torpedoes hit.

Meanwhile, shortly after 0700 hrs, Spruance had begun launching his strike against Nagumo, 175 miles distant, bearing 245 degrees to the southwest. Had *Chikuma* 'No 1' – the Type 0 Reconnaissance Seaplane flying the 77 degree search line – been more alert, it should have spotted Fletcher's TF-17 by 0630 hrs. But, apparently hampered by cloud cover, it had seen nothing. Then, at 0728 hrs, *Tone* 'No 4' sent a vaguely worded contact report of 'what appears to be ten enemy ships' bearing ten degrees, 240 miles north of Midway. The message was received on *Akagi's* bridge by 0740 hrs. This was way off the seaplane's base course, although at first nobody noticed.

Inexplicably, the crew had turned to port after flying only some 250 miles on its outbound leg. Whatever the reason for *Tone* 'No 4's' curious flight path, it was fortuitous, as the seaplane had stumbled upon

Spruance's TF-16. It would not have seen the vessels on its outward leg had the aircraft taken off on time and flown the proper course. Its contact report, however, mistakenly placed the ships some 53 miles north of their actual position.

At around 0745 hrs Nagumo ordered 'Prepare to attack enemy ships. Torpedo aeroplanes to retain torpedoes'. To *Tone* 'No 4' he shot back a message in the clear at 0747 hrs to 'ascertain ship type and maintain contact'. Mindful of Hara's mistake at Coral Sea in going after *Neosho* and *Sims*, Nagumo wanted confirmation.

With no doctrine of integrating separate air groups from different carriers into a single massed strike, as the Japanese performed with such consummate skill, each of Spruance's carriers launched two deck loads of aircraft sequentially, with each carrier air group operating independently. This consumed precious time, and risked loss of group cohesion once aloft. For its strike, *Hornet* launched ten escort F4Fs, 34 SBDs and six TBDs, followed by nine remaining TBDs in a second launch, completing the process at 0755 hrs.

The *Enterprise* launch was delayed when four SBDs broke down with mechanical problems. But 33 were already airborne (one later aborted), and the second deck load of ten F4Fs and 14 TBDs were being prepared for launch when, at 0740 hrs, Spruance's radio intelligence monitored *Tone* 'No 4's' transmission. Five minutes later, just as Nagumo reversed his earlier rearming order, Spruance ordered the airborne *Enterprise* SBDs to proceed. The vessel then completed its second launch by 0806 hrs.

Shortly after 0800 hrs, aeroplanes from Nagumo's Midway strike began to appear back over 1st Kido Butai, only to find it under attack by another wave of assailants from the island. While the Type 97s and most of the Type 99s circled in the distance, the escort Zero-sens joined the CAP fighters in battle. Six kanbaku from *Kaga*, including 2nd chutai leader Lt Toshio Watanabe and his veteran pilot WO Kazuyoshi Toiwatari, also joined the fray. Of 16 SBD-2s of VMSB-241, led by Maj Lofton R Henderson, that attempted a glide-bombing attack on *Hiryu*, only eight survived, four of them damaged beyond repair. They achieved several near misses, but no hits.

The Marine SBDs were followed shortly thereafter by 15 high-flying B-17s that dropped bombs on *Akagi*, *Hiryu* and *Soryu*. None of the Flying Fortresses were lost, but neither did they score any hits. Hard on their heels, at around 0820 hrs, came 11 antiquated SB2U-3s, the second echelon of VMSB-241. These attacked the battleship *Haruna* without effect and withdrew, losing two to fighters, while two others ditched.

At 0820 hrs, following various transmissions, *Tone* 'No 4' finally radioed 'enemy is accompanied by what appears to be one carrier to the rear'. *Soryu's* new Type 2 Carrier Reconnaissance aircraft departed at 0830 hrs to amplify the contact.

With the carriers heeling dangerously as they took evasive action against Midway's bombers, the feverish activity in the hangar decks of *Akagi* and *Kaga* to revert to torpedoes was far from complete. But the dive-bombers aboard *Hiryu* and *Soryu* were ready to go. 2nd Koku Sentai commander Tamon Yamaguchi sent a strongly worded signal to *Akagi*. 'Deem advisable we launch strike immediately with ordnance as is', but Nagumo did not respond. At the urging of senior air staff officer Minoru

Genda, the decision was made to complete rearming of the attack aeroplanes and launch a coordinated, mass attack according to doctrine. By now, most of the Zero-sens that had been allotted to escort the reserve force had been sent aloft to augment the CAP. Everyone on *Akagi's* bridge had just witnessed the sad fate of American bombers that had thrown themselves against 1st Kido Butai unescorted.

Furthermore, the returning aeroplanes of the Midway strike now circled impatiently, low on fuel, some damaged or with wounded aboard. The location of the enemy ships as reported by *Tone* 'No 4' was some 200 miles away. Confident that there was still time, Genda proposed to recover the Midway strike first. Its Zero-sens could then be used to escort the upcoming strike after being rearmed and refuelled. Nagumo and the rest of the staff concurred. But, the reported position of the American task force was in error. By now it was only 150 miles away, and its strike aeroplanes were already on their way.

The attacks from Midway finally abated at around 0840 hrs. A brief window of time now opened for Nagumo's carriers to spot and at least begin launching their strike before the American carrier aeroplanes arrived. However, that would force many from their own Midway strike to ditch while awaiting recovery – not a rational option. Landings began immediately. Still, three Type 97s (one from *Hiryu* and two from *Soryu*) ditched, although their crews were saved. Recovery of the Midway strike was largely completed by 0918 hrs, just as the first US carrier aeroplanes appeared. The precious window of time now closed irrevocably.

Meanwhile, after recovering his morning search and having closed range, Fletcher on *Yorktown* launched 17 SBDs, 12 TBDs and six F4Fs between 0838 hrs and 0907 hrs. He kept 17 SBDs in reserve.

As is well known, the first American carrier aeroplanes to arrive over the Japanese fleet were 15 TBDs of *Hornet's* VT-8. By 0935 hrs all had been shot down while attacking *Soryu* without scoring a hit, leaving a sole survivor swimming in the water. The rest of *Hornet's* squadrons, apparently searching for additional Japanese carriers, had headed west and missed the battle entirely, losing ten F4Fs and three SBDs in ditchings. Next, at 0940 hrs, came 14 TBDs of VT-6 from *Enterprise*. These attacked *Kaga*, but scored no hits, losing ten. Then, shortly after 1000 hrs, the dive-bombers from *Enterprise* arrived belatedly from the southwest. Coincidentally, the *Yorktown* squadrons approached from the southeast, the only US formation to maintain group integrity. This finally gave the American flyers a chance to make a coordinated attack.

Aboard Nagumo's carriers, activity became even more feverish as the aeroplanes just back from the Midway strike were prepared as a second wave against the US task force. Rearming of the first wave aboard *Akagi* and *Kaga* was nearing completion, the launch having originally been set for 1030 hrs. The waves of incoming enemy torpedo-bombers had caused great delay, however, with the flightdecks being kept busy cycling CAP fighters. The hangar decks were packed with fully armed and fuelled aeroplanes waiting for a 'lull in the storm' to spot and launch. Off-loaded ordnance lay scattered about the hangars, with no time to stow it properly below.

Lookouts spotted *Yorktown's* 12 TBDs of VT-3 shortly after 1000 hrs, but apparently missed the higher flying SBDs of VB-3 and the F4Fs of

VF-3. Nor did they see the approach of *Enterprise's* VB-6 and VS-6 from the southwest. Soon, the bulk of the CAP swarmed over VT-3. The attention of the ships' crew was also drawn to this new fight brewing at low altitude. Seven TBDs were 'splashed' before they could launch torpedoes. Five got close enough to drop their 'fish' against *Hiryu* at around 1035 hrs, but none exploded against its side. Only two TBDs made it out. Both would ditch before reaching home.

Then disaster struck Nagumo. While the Japanese were distracted by VT-3's attack, the SBDs had approached their targets unseen until they were nearly overhead. Lookouts saw them at the last minute, just as they went into their dives. Anti-aircraft batteries, still trained low against the torpedo attack, frantically cranked upward and began firing. But it was too late. The *Enterprise* SBDs scored against *Kaga* and *Akagi*, while those from *Yorktown* hit *Soryu*. In the space of five minutes, between 1023 hrs and 1028 hrs, *Kaga* and *Soryu* became blazing infernos as exploding fuel and ordnance from aeroplanes in the hangars added to the carnage. *Akagi's* fires also soon spiralled out of control. The Japanese CAP and anti-aircraft batteries managed to down no more than two or three SBDs, while one or two more ditched soon after bombing.

Casualties among the CAP Zero-sens had been heavy also. In action against the entire series of attacks from Midway and the US carriers that morning, no less than 17 IJN fighters had been lost, with 12 pilots killed.

Now only *Hiryu* remained. Nagumo and his staff departed the burning *Akagi* at 1048 hrs as Rear Adm Hiroaki Abe of 8th Sentai (heavy cruisers *Tone* and *Chikuma*) assumed temporary command of the fleet. At 1050 hrs, when Abe ordered Tamon Yamaguchi to attack the enemy, the latter had already decided to do so on his own initiative. Lt Michio Kobayashi's 18 Type 99 Carrier Bombers, together with six escort Zero-sens, were already on the flightdeck warming up. Rear Adm Yamaguchi came down from the bridge and shook hands with each individual airman about to depart. Tomonaga's attack aeroplanes, just back from Midway, were down in the hangars, deck crews frantically preparing them for a follow-up strike against the American ships. Upon transferring his flag to the light cruiser *Nagara*, Vice Adm Nagumo would signal his resumption of command at 1130 hrs.

Back at 0938 hrs, *Chikuma* 'No 5' had been launched as relief for *Tone* 'No 4'. At 1040 hrs it transmitted a contact report, having spotted part of TF-17 some 130 miles north of Midway. Meanwhile, at 1000 hrs, *Soryu's* Type 2 Carrier Reconnaissance aircraft had reached the position reported earlier by *Tone* 'No 4' and found nothing, even after searching 30 miles to the southeast. At 1008 hrs it started its return, but then came across an enemy carrier aeroplane at 1100 hrs and stalked it. Ten minutes later the Type 2 found what it was looking for and sent a contact report at 1130 hrs. The aeroplane eventually located all three American carriers, transmitting a second report at 1140 hrs. These signals, however, never reached Nagumo on *Nagara* or Yamaguchi aboard *Hiryu* due possibly to atmospheric disturbance. Although radio malfunction on the aircraft is usually given as the cause, records exist of other Japanese ships logging receipt of one or the other message.

At 1058 hrs, Kobayashi's 18 Type 99 Kanbaku departed on their fateful mission. The burning will of the entire fleet to even the score rode

This photograph shows *Hiryu* launching Type 99 dive-bombers during the Battle of Midway. One aircraft has just taken off and a second dive-bomber is already circling off the ship's port side. This shot is the only known operational image taken from the Japanese side during the Midway operation (*Yamato Museum*)

Lt Michio Kobayashi was the commander of *Hiryu's* Carrier Bomber Unit, which showed considerable skill and determination during the strike against *Yorktown* on the afternoon of 4 June. With *Hiryu* being the sole surviving Japanese carrier after the quick demise of *Akagi*, *Kaga* and *Soryu*, Kobayashi led the first retaliatory strike against the American carriers. The attack on *Yorktown* by *Hiryu's* Type 99s would be their finest hour. For Kobayashi, it would also be his last (*US Naval Historical Center*)

with them as funeral pyres of black smoke rose from *Kaga*, *Soryu* and *Akagi*. Kobayashi's own lead shotai of three and Lt Michiji Yamashita's lead shotai in the second chutai were armed with 242 kg land bombs for AA suppression, while the rest carried semi-armour piercing 250 kg ordinaries. At 1110 hrs, *Chikuma* 'No 5' reported the enemy carrier as bearing 070 degrees from base, only 90 miles away. At 1132 hrs it made radio contact directly with Kobayashi and transmitted a low frequency signal on which he could home in.

About halfway to the target, Kobayashi's formation came upon six American aircraft flying at low altitude. Thinking them to be torpedo bombers on their way to attack *Hiryu*, the Zero-sen escort pounced and damaged several, but two fighters were forced to head back, one with ammunition expended and the other so badly damaged that it was eventually forced to ditch. Their intended quarry had been *Enterprise's* dive-bombers trying to get home. Unable to locate the 'Big E' where they expected to find it, 18 SBDs eventually ditched. The four remaining Zero-sens chased after Kobayashi, but they now trailed behind the Type 99s, leaving the dive-bombers badly exposed.

Kobayashi sighted the American task force at 1155 hrs and began a climb to 3000 m, both his lead chutai and Yamashita's second chutai in echelon to the right in tight 'V-of-Vs' of nine aeroplanes each. They were confronted by CAP fighters of VF-3 while still some 15 to 20 miles out. First to fall was the kanbaku of FPO 1/c Hidemitsu Okamura (FPO 2/c Nobuyuki Nakao/pilot), the No 2 wingman in Kobayashi's second shotai on the extreme left of the lead 'V-of-V' being shot down by F4F ace Lt(jg) E Scott McCuskey. The latter then raked the other aeroplanes in the lead chutai from the rear and pulled ahead of the formation to the right. As he did so, Kobayashi and one

87

wingman turned into him in an aggressive move to fend off the F4Fs to allow some of the bombers to reach *Yorktown*, sacrificing formation discipline in the process. McCuskey now reversed course and barrelled through Yamashita's second chutai head-on, disrupting that formation.

In a matter of minutes, before the Zero-sens arrived, at least seven Type 99s fell to the guns of five F4Fs, while two or three damaged dive-bombers were forced to shed their bombs. One of them, apparently, was Kobayashi himself. Left with no other choice, he went to low altitude to observe the attack. His two wingmen and FPO 2/c Atsumi Tsuchiya, the No 2 man from third shotai, were the only survivors of Kobayashi's first chutai still lugging bombs. They approached *Yorktown* from astern.

At 1210 hrs, the first of them, believed to have been Kobayashi's No 2, FPO 1/c Kishichiro Yamada (FPO 1/c Shigeki Fukunaga/observer), opened the attack. Yamada held his dive down to a near suicidal 300 m, determined to score a hit regardless of his fate. Just as he reached the release point, anti-aircraft shells blasted the kanbaku into three chunks, but Yamada had aimed true. His instantaneously-fused land bomb tumbled end over end and detonated on contact abaft the midships elevator, mowing down men at the 1.1-in guns aft of *Yorktown*'s island, opening an 11-ft hole in the flightdeck and starting a fire among three SBDs in the hangar deck below. Yamada and Fukunaga splashed in *Yorktown*'s wake close aboard the starboard quarter. Observing the reddish column of fire from their bomb shoot 20 m into the air, Kobayashi transmitted 'enemy carrier burning' at 1211 hrs.

Next came Kobayashi's No 3, FPO 3/c Hideo Sakai (pilot) and FPO 3/c Takeichi Yamaguchi (observer), who suffered a similar fate. Their bomb detonated on contact with the ship's wake and peppered *Yorktown*'s fantail with shrapnel. The last of the first chutai trio to dive was Atsumi Tsuchiya (FPO 2/c Hayata Egami/observer). Approaching from the port quarter, he made a steep 75-degree dive from 3000 m. His ordinary bomb near-missed just off the stern, but he made good his escape above the wave tops.

This left four survivors from second chutai approaching from the south. They spread out in a ragged 'crane's wing' formation to attack from different angles to starboard, as *Yorktown* turned sharply away to port. FPO 1/c Sadao Matsumoto (pilot) and FPO 1/c Nobusato Yasuda (observer), sole survivors of the land bomb-equipped first shotai

*Yorktown* under attack from Kobayashi's dive-bombers on 4 June 1942. The aeroplane diving on the carrier from astern is probably that of FPO 2/c Atsumi Tsuchiya (commander/pilot) and FPO 2/c Hayata Egami (observer) (*NA 80-G-32310 via Mike Wenger*)

One of *Hiryu's* Type 99s was photographed from the heavy cruiser USS *Astoria* (CA-34) after it had made its attack on *Yorktown* (*NA 80-G-32294 via Mike Wenger*)

of second chutai, rounded the vessel's stern and attacked from the port quarter. Their bomb missed astern. Similarly shifting their attack to the port quarter, however, WO Iwao Nakazawa (pilot) and second shotai leader Special Duty Ens Shimematsu Nakayama (observer/commander) scored a hit squarely amidships with their ordinary bomb at 1214 hrs. This weapon detonated deep inside the hull, damaging the uptakes to the boilers and extinguishing the fires in all but one. *Yorktown* slowed to six knots as black smoke billowed from its amidships wound.

A minute later came third shotai leader WO Shizuo Nakagawa (FPO 1/c Ryuji Otomo/observer) who made a glide-bombing run aiming for the carrier's starboard bow. His bomb penetrated the forward elevator, starting several small fires, and forced the flooding of a magazine. The last to dive was FPO 1/c Tetsuo Seo (FPO 3/c Chikayoshi Murakami/observer), Nakayama's No 2, who planted a near miss close aboard *Yorktown's* starboard beam. All four of the second chutai attackers successfully withdrew at low level.

Michio Kobayashi never returned. Intent on observing the attack, he and his observer WO Yoshinori Ono evidently fell victim to two F4Fs of *Enterprise's* VF-6, part of the CAP reinforcement sent up from TF-16 to assist *Yorktown*. A total of 13 Type 99s were lost in the attack on Fletcher's carrier. As the last shotai leader, Shizuo Nakagawa circled for 30 minutes at the post-strike rendezvous, observing results and waiting for stragglers who never came. At 1245 hrs he radioed 'Enemy carrier burning. No friendly aircraft in sight. I am returning'.

Meanwhile, after fleeing eastward from pursuing enemy fighters, *Chikuma* 'No 5' had discovered TF-16, and had reported the new contact at 1220 hrs, shortly after Kobayashi had reported disabling his target. The Japanese now knew the location of two enemy carriers. One down, one to go, figured Yamaguchi.

*Hiryu's* second strike, consisting of ten Type 97s and six Zero-sens, departed at 1331 hrs with orders to attack the new carrier reported by *Chikuma* 'No 5'. Joichi Tomonaga led the strike, still flying his aeroplane with its empty holed wing tank.

With *Hiryu's* flightdeck cleared, *Soryu's* Type 2 Carrier Reconnaissance aircraft came in to land. From its crew, Yamaguchi finally received definite news of the presence of three US carriers. The survivors of the first strike landed soon after at 1338 hrs. Only five Type 99s returned, including one damaged beyond repair. Among the Zero-sens, only Lt Yasuhiro Shigematsu, the escort leader, came back from the battle over *Yorktown*. Three had been lost in duels with the F4Fs in exchange for just one US fighter. The losses staggered even the redoubtable Yamaguchi.

Between 1340 hrs and 1345 hrs, *Chikuma* 'No 5' sent updated reports on the position of TF-16, but then fell victim to two F4Fs from *Enterprise* at 1409 hrs.

By 1400 hrs repairs aboard *Yorktown* were going well. Following the dive-bombing attack the vessel had gone dead in the water, but the fires were quickly extinguished or contained and the carrier began to move again under its own power as three boilers came back online. At 1430 hrs Tomonaga's formation spotted *Yorktown*. Although the location was further north than expected, the carrier showed no outward signs of distress. Mistaking it for the newly discovered second carrier, Tomonaga attacked. Five attack aeroplanes fell to defending F4Fs, including Tomonaga's. Nevertheless, by 1444 hrs, the remaining aircraft had put two torpedoes into *Yorktown's* port side amidships, while the escorting Zero-sens did their best to fend off the American CAP, shooting down four fighters from VF-3.

*Yorktown* lost all power and developed a list to port that eventually reached almost 30 degrees, with the rudder jammed 15 degrees to port. Fifteen minutes after the torpedo attack, *Yorktown's* captain decided to abandon ship. Five Type 97s and four Zero-sens survived the battle and returned to *Hiryu*, the attack aeroplanes and two of the fighters landing by 1545 hrs.

Tamon Yamaguchi had, meanwhile, been busy preparing a third strike with whatever aeroplanes he could muster. Seeing the heavy losses suffered by his first strike, he decided to postpone the third strike to a dusk attack. He hurried repairs to damaged aircraft and ordered food and rest for his exhausted flyers. At 1630 hrs the third strike launch was set for 1800 hrs, with five kanbaku, four attack aeroplanes and ten fighters.

Then, shortly before 1645 hrs, CAP Zero-sens spotted incoming SBDs. Without effective voice radios in their cockpits, no word reached *Hiryu*. Lookouts in the fleet failed to see the enemy aeroplanes as they approached from the west, out of the sun. Finally, at 1701 hrs, the SBDs were suddenly discovered overhead, about to go into their dives.

*Yorktown* after Kobayashi's dive-bomber attack. The ship is dead in the water and burning from the hit in the stack uptakes. However, in a short period of time, its crew would control all fires and restore speed to 19 knots (*US Naval Historical Center*)

The end of *Hiryu*. Hit by four 1000 lb bombs from *Enterprise's* SBDs in the late afternoon of 4 June, *Hiryu* is seen here on the morning of the 5th, adrift and smoking, although still afloat. It would sink some two hours after this photograph was taken (*NHC via Jonathan Parshall*)

Sixteen minutes earlier, two SBD scouts from *Yorktown* had located *Hiryu*. *Enterprise* had launched 25 SBDs (including 14 refugees from *Yorktown*) by 1542 hrs, with *Hornet* following with 16 more at 1604 hrs. Minus three aborts, 38 SBDs had gone after the remaining Japanese carrier and its attendants.

In a desperate bid to save their sole surviving carrier, defending Zero-sens followed the SBDs down in the dive and destroyed three of them. However, at 1703 hrs, the remaining Dauntlesses plastered *Hiryu* with four 1000 lb bombs forward of the bridge, demolishing the forward flightdeck and hurling part of the forward elevator back against the bridge.

Despite all four carriers now having been knocked out, both Nagumo and Yamamoto were initially determined to continue the battle with a surface action against the Americans. By 2130 hrs Nagumo realised this was impractical, and Yamamoto finally relented around midnight. The capture of Midway was formally cancelled at 0255 hrs on 5 June.

Desperate attempts to fight the fires aboard *Kaga*, *Soryu* and *Akagi* had continued all day on the 4th, but to no avail. *Soryu* was scuttled by three torpedoes from the destroyer *Isokaze*, sinking at 1913 hrs. *Kaga's* fierce fires had consumed it almost down to the waterline by the time the destroyer *Hagikaze* put the vessel out of its misery at 1925 hrs. *Akagi* continued to linger, but was finally ordered scuttled the next morning, sinking by 0520 hrs on the 5th. Fire fighting on *Hiryu* continued throughout the night, but 'abandon ship' was ordered at 0315 hrs on the 5th. At 0510 hrs the destroyer *Makigumo* sent one torpedo into the carrier's starboard side and departed. *Hiryu*, however, remained afloat, finally sinking well after sunrise at around 0915 hrs.

Rear Adm Tamon Yamaguchi shared the fate of his flagship, together with its skipper, Capt Tomeo Kaku. The captains of *Kaga* and *Soryu* had also gone down with their ships.

Surprisingly, only 29 carrier airmen were lost aboard ship or in the water. Seven were kanbaku men. After returning from the Midway strike as dive-bomber leader, Lt Shoichi Ogawa had been grievously wounded during the SBD attack. He died aboard *Kaga*, waving and shouting encouragement to his men in the water. Ogawa would receive a posthumous double promotion to the rank of commander. Kanbaku observer Ryuji Otomo had returned after surviving the first strike on *Yorktown*, only to die aboard *Hiryu* that afternoon. Struggling in the water, with death and destruction all around him, *Soryu's* Type 99 pilot FPO 3/c Sadao Endo raised his service pistol to his temple and pulled the trigger.

The final curtain on the Midway drama did not ring down for another two days. The heavy cruisers *Mikuma* and *Mogami* collided in the early hours of 5 June and *Mikuma* was sunk by SBDs the next day. The early hours of 6 June found *Yorktown* still afloat with a salvage party back onboard. However, the Japanese submarine I-168 torpedoed both the carrier and the destroyer USS *Hammann* (DD-412) that afternoon. *Yorktown* finally sank at 0501 hrs on 7 June.

The IJN lost more than 3000 men in the Battle of Midway. Contrary to popular belief, however, only 121 were airmen. The Americans lost 188 flyers. But the huge loss of highly trained mechanics, armourers and flightdeck crew, not to mention the loss of four fleet carriers and their sailors, was a devastating blow from which the IJN would never recover.

## 1

**Type 99 Carrier Bomber (D3A1) Model 11 '9-257' of 14th Kokutai, Nanning, South China, March 1940**
Based in south China, the dive-bomber chutai of 14th Ku became the first operational unit to receive the new 11-Shi Carrier Bomber in November 1939, a month prior to the aeroplane's service adoption as the Type 99 Carrier Bomber (D3A1). Transition to the new type was completed by March 1940. This aircraft is depicted here in a silver paint finish and sports a black anti-glare panel that covers the entire engine cowling, with a curved demarcation line to the front of the windscreen – a style of application characteristic of all Type 99 Kanbaku until the advent of dark green uppersurface camouflage in early 1942. The red tail assembly was mandated for all operational IJN aircraft, except trainers, from 5 June 1933 as a visual aid in locating downed machines, serving much the same function as the chrome yellow wings on prewar US Navy aircraft. Red tails were also applied to trainers from 30 May 1935 until spring 1939, when they were painted overall orange-yellow based on a directive dated 29 December 1938. The Arabic numeral 9 on the vertical fin is the unit code assigned to 14th Ku upon its formation on 6 April 1938. All carrier bomber (i.e. dive-bomber) aircraft in the IJN were assigned individual aircraft numbers in the 200s range from 1 October 1936 onward. The white stripe bordered in red on the rear fuselage is the senchi hyoshiki, or 'combat zone marking' (often translated as 'combat stripe'). It was applied, beginning in 1937 with the start of the China War, to aeroplanes in combat zones for quick recognition of friendly aircraft. '9-257' is shown here carrying a Provisional Designation Type 98 No 25 Land Bomb, a 250 kg class weapon designed for use against land targets. It weighed 242 kg and packed a 96.6 kg explosive charge.

## 2

**Type 99 Carrier Bomber (D3A1) Model 11 '3-222' of 12th Kokutai, Hankow, Central China, June 1940**
12th Ku served in central China, its kanbaku chutai receiving the Type 99 Carrier Bomber in early May 1940. Originally assigned the Roman alphabet letter 'S' as a unit marking, 12th Ku was given the Arabic numeral '3' as its code in October 1937 when air units stationed in China were issued with sequentially allotted numerical codes. Note the red flash on the undercarriage wheel cover – a marking first applied to the Type 99 by 12th Kokutai. The flash was also applied to the inside surface of the cover, but was truncated and did not extend to a point as on the outside. 14th Ku in South China did not apply the flash marking to its kanbaku.

## 3

**Type 99 Carrier Bomber (D3A1) Model 11 'AI-205' aboard *Akagi*, Japan, April 1941**
Upon its formation on 10 April 1941, 1st Air Fleet (Dai-ichi Koku Kantai) instituted a tail code system reflecting the standard format then in use for shipboard aircraft serving under Combined Fleet. This consisted of a Roman alphabet letter indicating the sentai ('warship division' for units afloat in the case of the IJN, not to be confused with the same term used by the Imperial Japanese Army Air Corps), followed by a Roman numeral denoting the ship's position within the sentai. The letter 'A' indicated 1st Koku Sentai, while Roman numeral 'I' indicated the carrier *Akagi* – the first vessel within the koku sentai according to the administrative order of battle (which was not necessarily the same as making the vessel a flagship). Note that the term koku sentai is usually translated as 'carrier division' in the case of a formation of aircraft carriers and 'air flotilla' in the case of a land-based aircraft organisation, despite the term meaning exactly the same in the original Japanese. A system of colour-coded stripes on the rear fuselage would become a standard part of the unit marking system within 1st Air Fleet, with *Akagi*'s aeroplanes coming to sport a single red stripe. This marking had yet to be applied to 'AI-205' in April 1941.

## 4

**Type 99 Carrier Bomber (D3A1) Model 11 'AII-234' aboard *Kaga*, Japan, August 1941**
As the second vessel in 1st Koku Sentai, carrier *Kaga* was assigned 'AII' as a unit code. Fuselage stripes are now in evidence, 1st Koku Sentai using red as a colour and *Kaga* having two stripes to signify it being the second vessel. The style of demarcation of the red colour along the vertical fin was unique to *Kaga*, and differs from the standard style applied to the examples previously illustrated from 12th and 14th Ku and *Akagi*. Also, the red flash on the undercarriage wheel cover extends to the rear, even on the inside surface, unlike those applied to aircraft of 12th Ku. Carrier-based Type 99s usually had the last two digits of the individual aircraft number painted in small figures at the very front of the wheel covers, typically inside the red flash. This allowed quick identification of each aircraft within a carrier's hangar deck

## 5

**Type 99 Carrier Bomber (D3A1) Model 11 '9-273' of 14th Kokutai, Saigon, French Indochina, August 1941**
During the summer of 1941, Type 99 Kanbaku were painted overall light olive grey, and red tails were discontinued. The 'combat stripe', however,

seen here thinly outlined in red, was still in evidence on the aircraft of 14th Ku in French Indochina. This marking was rapidly phased out in the IJN during 1940-41, but remained a standard feature of JAAF aircraft in combat theatres throughout the Pacific War.

## 6

### Type 99 Carrier Bomber (D3A1) Model 11 'EI-238' of Lt Cdr Kakuichi Takahashi aboard *Shokaku*, December 1941–January 1942

The aircraft of Shokaku Hikotaicho (i.e. flying group leader) Kakuichi Takahashi is shown here in the finish and markings it carried from autumn 1941 through to Operation *R* (the invasion of the Bismarck Archipelago) in January 1942. Roman alphabet letter 'E' was the code assigned to 5th Koku Sentai (carriers *Zuikaku* and *Shokaku*), while Roman numeral 'I' identified *Shokaku* as the first vessel within the koku sentai, having been the first of the two carriers to be commissioned and assigned to that organisation. *Shokaku* maintained this position under the administrative order of battle, although Rear Adm Chuichi Hara, the sentai commander, flew his flag aboard *Zuikaku*, thus making the latter vessel the tactical flagship during this period. 5th Koku Sentai used the colour white for the rear fuselage stripes on its aircraft, with the carrier *Shokaku* applying a single stripe as the first vessel. The three horizontal stripes on the tail (one above and two beneath the tail code on the Type 99 Kanbaku) denote a hikotaicho. The aircraft of a buntaicho (squad leader in reference to personnel, and chutaicho for an aerial formation of aircraft) sported two stripes, both beneath the tail code in the case of the Type 99 Kanbaku. A single stripe (also applied beneath the tail code on Type 99s) indicated a shotaicho (flight leader). The colour of the unit code and individual aeroplane number displayed on aircraft tails was determined at fleet level. With discontinuation of red tails, these markings were carried in red for all aircraft within 1st Air Fleet. Note the pointed blade motif used as a flash marking on the undercarriage wheel covers, a style unique to the dive-bombers of 5th Koku Sentai. On these aircraft, the last two digits of the individual aeroplane number were carried just above the point where the front tips of the blade motif, applied to the inner and outer sides of the wheel cover, converged. Takahashi's aircraft is shown here armed with a Type 98 No 25 Land Bomb Model 1, the ordnance carried at the time of his opening attack on NAS Ford Island, Pearl Harbor, as overall leader of the first attack wave dive-bombers. The 'Provisional Designation' prefix for this ordnance, which still applied in 1940, was dropped with its formal service adoption on 29 August 1941. In a postwar article in a special issue of *Rekishi Dokuhon* magazine, Takashi Nakagawa, junior dive-bomber buntaicho aboard *Hiryu* at the time of the Pearl Harbor attack, stated that, for the Hawaiian operation, the aircraft of dive-bomber leaders down to buntaicho level displayed uniquely colourful finishes and markings. According to Nakagawa, these special schemes were adopted as quick visual aids in reformation, since dive-bombers often became widely separated after their attack. The schemes thus fulfilled a function roughly similar to the gaudy paint schemes applied to US Eighth Air Force formating aircraft. Nakagawa's testimony records that the aircraft of Lt Cdr Egusa, *Soryu* Hikotaicho and overall leader of the second wave dive-bombers at Pearl Harbor, sported a rough, mottled pattern of red paint on its uppersurfaces, and was nicknamed 'ja-ja uma' (a ceremonial horse, traditionally adorned in red in Japan). Similarly, according to Nakagawa, the aircraft of Lt Cdr Takahashi, *Shokaku* Hikotaicho and leader of the first wave dive-bombers at Pearl Harbor, had its uppersurfaces painted a bright orange and was nicknamed 'dora neko' (alley cat). He goes on to state that the special paint scheme on his own aircraft was rather modest by comparison, consisting of 'a streamlined green flash marking along the fuselage on a white background'. Independent research by this author, however, casts doubt on the complete accuracy of Nakagawa's remarks. In a telephone interview with the author on 6 December 2006, WO Hachiro Miyashita, who served as crew chief for Lt Cdr Takahashi's aircraft aboard *Shokaku*, and was thus personally responsible for all aspects of the aeroplane's upkeep, stated emphatically that Takahashi's aircraft never wore anything other than standard finish. I have chosen, therefore, to depict Takahashi's aircraft according to Miyashita's testimony, which I consider to be the most reliable. Similarly, correspondence by the author with Zenji Abe (junior kanbaku buntaicho aboard *Akagi* at Pearl Harbor) and Kenji Hori (kanbaku pilot aboard *Zuikaku* at the time of the operation) indicate that command dive-bombers aboard those carriers sported no special finish or markings other than the standard command stripes on the tail. As of this writing, therefore, it is this author's opinion that, if special markings were in fact used at Pearl Harbor, they were limited to the command dive-bombers of 2nd Koku Sentai (*Soryu* and *Hiryu*).

## 7

### Type 99 Carrier Bomber (D3A1) Model 11 'BI-231' of Lt Cdr Takashige Egusa aboard *Soryu*, October–December 1941

In contrast to the sole, contested, testimony of Takashi Nakagawa concerning the colour scheme on Kakuichi Takahashi's aeroplane, there are several independent, and consistent, eyewitness accounts regarding Takashige Egusa's red-painted aircraft. As recorded by author Shiro Mori in *Kaigun Sentokitai* Vol 2 p 80, Cdr Mitsuo Fuchida first used the nickname 'ja-ja uma' in reference to Egusa's mount during pre-Pearl Harbor training in Kyushu. Among others, Tatsuo Itazu, *Hiryu* dive-bomber observer at Pearl Harbor, confirmed the red colour pattern on Egusa's aircraft in an interview given to camouflage and markings researcher Hitoshi Yoshimura (*Model Art Magazine* No 225, January 1984). Consensus among eyewitnesses describes a complex mottled pattern in red, possibly mixed with yellow, on the fuselage of Egusa's Type 99, which, from a distance, appeared solidly red. It should be noted, however, that, unlike the other colour profiles in this book, Egusa's aircraft depicted here is not based on direct photo evidence or contemporary records. Furthermore, the individual aircraft number '231' is associated with Egusa only from a flight roster during training for the Hawaiian operation. Thus, although it is likely that he flew the same aircraft at Pearl Harbor, there is no hard evidence for this at this time. The letter 'B' indicates 2nd Koku Sentai, with the Roman numeral 'I' denoting *Soryu* as first vessel. The rear fuselage stripe colour for 2nd Koku Sentai was blue, with *Soryu's* aircraft carrying a single stripe indicating first vessel within the koku sentai. Egusa's aircraft carries the three tail stripes of a hikotaicho, and is seen here armed with a Type 99 No 25 Ordinary Bomb Model 1 – the ordnance it carried for the Pearl Harbor attack. A 250 kg class ordinary bomb (semi-armour piercing) for use against warships, this bomb was thinner than the Type 98 No 25 Land Bomb used by the first wave dive-bombers from 5th Koku Sentai. It weighed 251 kg and carried an explosive charge of 56.5 kg. This was considerably less than the charge in the Type 98 land bomb, but it had a harder and thicker outer casing for penetration of warship armour.

## 8
### Type 99 Carrier Bomber (D3A1) Model 11 'AI-207' of Lt(jg) Keizo Obuchi aboard *Akagi*, January–April 1942

Lt(jg) Obuchi's kanbaku is shown here as it appeared during the period from Operation *R* in January 1942 through Operation *C*, the Indian Ocean raid, in April 1942. Unlike those of *Akagi's* 1st dive-bomber chutai, the Type 99s of the vessel's 2nd dive-bomber chutai did not carry any flash markings on their undercarriage wheel covers during 1941 (including for the Hawaiian operation), but applied them prior to departing Japan for Operation *R* in January 1942. The style used was a straight horizontal band that carried back to about the middle of the wheel cover, before converging in a straight-line taper to a point at the rear, unlike the smoothly curved flash markings seen on the Type 99s of 12th Ku and aboard *Kaga* and *Soryu*. The last one or two digits of the individual aeroplane number that had previously been painted on the bottom front lip of the engine cowling in the 2nd chutai were now moved to the front of each wheel cover within the flash. Obuchi's aircraft also displays the single tail stripe of a shotaicho (flight leader). Black and white photo evidence appears to show this stripe in a markedly darker shade than the fuselage hinomaru, and it is thus depicted here in black, although it could possibly have been applied in red too.

## 9
### Type 99 Carrier Bomber (D3A1) Model 11 'AII-256' of F 1/c Shinsaku Yamakawa aboard *Kaga*, December 1941–March 1942

F 1/c Yamakawa's Type 99 is seen here in standard *Kaga* markings and early war finish. This aircraft was a presentation machine, as evidenced by the inscription on the rear fuselage superimposed over the double red stripes. This read *Hokoku* 522 (*Dai 55 Zen Nippon Go*), denoting that it was the 522nd aircraft presented to the IJN and the 55th machine purchased by nationwide subscription. In this particular case the aeroplane was purchased by student donations from girls' schools throughout Japan. Yamakawa flew this aircraft from Pearl Harbor through to the anti-shipping sweep south of Java in March 1942. All presentation weapons, including aircraft, for the IJN were referred to as hokoku machines, while those for the Imperial Army were called aikoku. Both terms may be translated as 'patriot' or 'patriotism', although the literal translation for hokoku is 'service to country', while aikoku is 'love of country'. Yamakawa's dive-bomber also sports a different style of flash marking seen on the wheel covers of some *Kaga* aeroplanes, with the upper and lower edges converging in a straight line instead of a curve. The difference between the two styles probably reflects separate maintenance buntai assignments for the aircraft. Finally, note the white stencilling block on the side of the engine cowling. This served as a handily placed checklist for Type 99 engine maintenance personnel.

## 10
### Type 99 Carrier Bomber (D3A1) Model 11 'BI-259' aboard *Soryu*, December 1941

This dive-bomber from *Soryu* is depicted in standard markings and finish for December 1941. At Pearl Harbor the aircraft participated in the second wave assault, crewed by FPO 3/c Hiroe Mizutani (observer/commander) and F 1/c Sadao Endo (pilot), and it dived on the battleship *California*.

## 11
### Type 99 Carrier Bomber (D3A1) Model 11 'BII-214' of FPO 2/c Yoshio Shimizu aboard *Hiryu*, December 1941

The usual mount of FPO 3/c Tatsuo Itazu, this aeroplane was manned by FPO 2/c Yoshio Shimizu (observer/commander) and FPO 2/c Isamu Kiyomura (pilot) during the second wave attack at Pearl Harbor. The aircraft was hit by flak over 'Battleship Row' and is believed to have subsequently crashed at Aiea Heights. It carries the tail code for the carrier *Hiryu*, 'BII', as well as two blue rear fuselage stripes, signifying it as the second vessel in 2nd Koku Sentai. Note the style of flash marking on the wheel cover used by *Hiryu* dive-bombers – a straight line convergence similar to that seen on F 1/c Yamakawa's aircraft from *Kaga* (Colour Plate 9).

**12**

**Type 99 Carrier Bomber (D3A1) Model 11 'EI-204' aboard *Shokaku*, December 1941–January 1942**
This aircraft was flown by a shotai leader from *Shokaku*, hence the single tail stripe. Note also the distinctive blade-shaped flash marking used on the Type 99s of 5th Koku Sentai. The aeroplane is shown carrying a 60 kg class Type 99 No 6 Ordinary Bomb Model 1 (total weight 62.8 kg, with a 30 kg explosive charge) beneath each wing for a routine anti-submarine patrol.

**13**

**Type 99 Carrier Bomber (D3A1) Model 11 'EII-206' aboard *Zuikaku*, December 1941–January 1942**
Presentation aircraft *Hokoku* 525 (*Dai 58 Zen Nippon Go*), this machine was the 58th aircraft donated by nationwide subscription. Other presentation aeroplanes were often donated by specific organisations, companies or wealthy individuals. Tail code 'EII' and two white rear fuselage stripes indicate assignment to *Zuikaku*. The aircraft carries the single tail stripe of a shotaicho. Although the well-known photograph of this aircraft shows a dark stripe, this is believed to be a later addition superimposed on the negative itself, and that the actual colour was white. The aeroplane is believed to have had its wheel covers painted red, onto which a blade-shaped flash marking was applied in white. This was an unusual departure from the standard red flash seen on all other examples.

**14**

**Type 99 Carrier Bomber (D3A1) Model 11 'BI-263' of FPO 2/c Takeo Yamazaki aboard *Soryu*, Staring Bay, Celebes, March 1942**
Photo evidence and veteran testimony indicate that when 2nd Koku Sentai (*Soryu* and *Hiryu*) departed Japan on 12 January 1942, its kanbaku carried dark green uppersurface camouflage. On this early application of the camouflage, the engine cowling remains black, although the light olive grey undersurface finish was extended to cover the bottom portion of the cowling. Note the dark green paint also applied to the front half of the wheel covers. When the carriers of 1st Koku Sentai (*Akagi* and *Kaga*) and 5th Koku Sentai (*Zuikaku* and *Shokaku*) had sortied for Operation R (the capture of Rabaul and Kavieng) earlier in January, photo

evidence shows that their Type 99s still retained the overall light olive grey finish seen during the Hawaiian operation. Joining 2nd Koku Sentai and continuing to participate in the southern advance during the raid on Darwin in February and the sweep south of Java in March, the dive-bombers of 1st Koku Sentai remained in light olive grey finish, while those of 2nd Koku Sentai already sported dark green uppersurfaces. *Kaga* then headed back to Japan for repairs. Meanwhile, the carriers of 5th Koku Sentai had returned to Japan following Operation R. By the time they rejoined Nagumo's fleet at Staring Bay, in the Celebes, in March 1942 for the Indian Ocean raid, their dive-bombers had been given dark green uppersurface camouflage during their stay in home waters. As the only carrier that had not returned to Japan following Operation R, *Akagi* became the sole vessel whose kanbaku remained in light olive grey during the Indian Ocean raid of April 1942. Seen here is the kanbaku piloted by FPO 2/c Takeo Yamazaki at Kendari, in the Celebes, where the carrier flight echelons were based while the ships of Kido Butai anchored at Staring Bay prior to the Indian Ocean raid.

**15**

**Type 99 Carrier Bomber (D3A1) Model 11 'EI-208' aboard *Shokaku* during the Battle of the Coral Sea, May 1942**
As noted earlier, the dive-bombers of 5th Koku Sentai sported dark green uppersurface camouflage before the time of the Coral Sea battle. The red tail code and individual aeroplane number of 1st Air Fleet remain, now outlined in white for better visibility against the green camouflage. Note also the retention of the distinctive blade-shaped red flash marking on the wheel covers.

**Back Cover**

**Type 99 Carrier Bomber (D3A1) Model 11 '35-201' of 35th Kokutai, Makassar, Celebes, May 1942**
Unlike the majority of combat air units under Combined Fleet, the garrison units activated to operate under assignment to various special base forces (tokubetsu konkyochi-tai) in the newly captured territories were simply given codes that directly reflected the unit's numerical designation. This aircraft of 35th Ku sports a shotaicho stripe on the tail. It carries one 30 kg class Type 99 No 3 Exercise Bomb Model 1 under each wing.

# INDEX

References to illustrations are shown in **bold**. Plates are shown with page and caption locators in brackets.

Abe, Lt Zenji 33, **35**, **57**, 57, 58, 60, 77, 78, 79, 93
Aichi 7; 11-Shi Carrier-based Bomber (AM-17 – *later* Type 99 Carrier Bomber Model 11) **9**, 9–13, **10**, **12**, **13**; Type 94 Carrier-based Bomber (D1A1) 7–8; Type 96 Carrier Bomber (D1A2) **7**, 8, 17; Type 99 Carrier Bomber (D3A2) Model 22: 13–14, **14**
Aichi Type 99 Carrier Bomber (D3A1) Model 11: **4**, **14**, **15**, **16**, **17**, **30**, **32**, **50**, **89**; '3-222' **2**(41, 92); '9-257' **1**(41, 92); '9-273' **5**(42, 92–93); '33-203' **53**; '35-201' **53**, **95**; 'AI-202' **35**; 'AI-205' **17**, **3**(41,

92); 'AI-207' **8**(43, 94), **56**; 'AI-208' **22**, 36; 'AI-254' **49**; 'AII-234' **4**(42, 92); 'AII-252' **21**; 'AII-256' **9**(43, 94); 'BI-231' **7**(43, 93–94); 'BI-259' **10**(44, 94); 'BI-263' **14**(45, 95); 'BII-214' 32, **11**(44, 94); 'EI-204' **12**(44, 95), **48**; 'EI-208' **15**(45, 95), **71**; 'EI-238' **6**(42, 93), **47**; 'EII-203' **38**; 'EII-206' **13**(45, 95), **46**; *Kaga* air group **26**, **27**, **32**, **33**, **34**; specifications 13; *see also* Aichi: 11-Shi Carrier-based Bomber
Aleutians operation (1942) 76, 77–79
Arima, Lt Keiichi 15
Asahi, FPO 3/c Naga-aki 34
Australian Air Force, Royal (RAAF) 46, 47, 51

Bando, FPO 3/c Toshiaki 36–37
Brassfield, Lt(jg) Arthur J 72
Brown, 2Lt Harry W 35, 36

Ceylon raids (1942) 55–57, **56**, 59
Chihaya, Lt Takehiko 23, **31**, 32, 50, 57
China, war in **7**, 8, 15–16, 18, 19, 20
Coral Sea, Battle of the (1942) **15**(45, 95), **70**, 70–75, **71**, **72**, **73**, 77, 84

Dains, 2Lt John L 35
Darwin attack (1942) **49**, 49–51, **50**, **51**

Egusa, Lt Cdr Takashige 21, 26, 30, 34, 40, **7**(43, 93–94), 50, 52, 57, 58, 60, **61**, 61
Ema, Lt Tamotsu 27, 56, 60, 62, 69, 72, 73, 74
Endo, FPO 3/c Sadao 91, 94

Fletcher, Rear Adm Frank 'Black Jack' 39, 40, 64, 65–66, 69, 70, 75, 80, 81, 82, 85
Fuchida, Cdr Mitsuo 20, 21, 26, 27, 28, 46, 47, 49, 50, 52, 56, 57, 81, 93
Fujita, Lt Hisayoshi 28, 56–57

Gaylor, Lt Noel 73
Genda, Cdr Minoru 19, 84–85
Gomei, Tokuichiro 7, 9
Goto, FPO 2/c Hajime 35

Halsey, Vice Adm William 64, 80
Hara, Rear Adm Chuichi **46**, 63, 65, 66, 68, 70, 74, 84
Hawaiian operation (1941) 19–24, return voyage 39–40 *see also* Pearl Harbor attack
Heinkel 7, 10; He 66: 7; He 70 Blitz 9
Hirashima, FPO 2/c Fumio 36–37

Ikeda, Lt Masai 31, 51
Inagaki, FPO 1/c Toshio 27, 69
Inoue, Vice Adm Shigeyoshi 39, 63, 64, 69, 75
Ishizuka, FPO 2/c Shigeo 67
Itazu, FPO 3/c Tatsuo 24, 31–32, 37, 52, 93–94

Japanese Navy, Imperial (IJN)
   8-Shi Carrier-based Special Bomber 6, 7
   11-Shi Carrier-based Bomber 8–9 *see also* Aichi 11-Shi Carrier-based Bomber; Nakajima 11-Shi Carrier-based Bomber
   air fleets: Eleventh 20, 22; First 17, 18–19, 20, 21, 20, 22
   air groups: *Akagi* 6, **17**, **22**, 25, 26, 30, 32–33, **35**, 37, 38, **3**(41, 92), **8**(43, 94), 46, 47, 49, 50, 52, 54, 55, **56**, 57, 58, 59, 60, 81, 82–83; *Hiryu* 18, 19, 24, 25, 26, 30, 31–32, 35, 38, 40, **11**(44, 94), 48, 49, 51, 52–53, 54, 55, 57, 58, 59, 60, 81, 86–87, **87**, 88–89, **89**, 90; *Junyo* 77, 78; *Kaga* 6, **21**, 25, **27**, 30, **32**, **33**, **34**, 34, 36, 38, 4(42, 92), **9**(43, 94), 46, 47, 49–50, 51, 52, 81, 82–83, 84; *Ryujo* 7, 77, 78, 79; *Shokaku* **4**, 23, 25, 26, 27, 28–29, 38, **6**(42, 93), **12**(44, 95), **15**(45, 95), 46–47, **47**, **48**, 55, 56, 57, 59–61, 65, 66–67, 68, 69, 70–71, **71**, **72**, 72, 73; *Soryu* 18, 19, 25, 26, 30–31, 34–35, 38, 39, 40, 49, **7**(43, 93–94), **10**(44, 94), **14**(45, 95), 49, 50, 51, 52–53, 54, 55, 57, 58, 59, 60, 61, 81, 84; *Zuikaku* 22–23, 24, 25, 26, 27, 28, 29, **38**, 38, **13**(45, 95), 46, 47, 55, 56, 57, 59, 60, 65, 67, 68, 69, 70, 71, 72–73
   aircraft designations 8, 13–14
   fleets: Combined 17, 19–20, 22, 39, 46, 48, 54, 63, 75, 76, 77, 80, 82; 1st and 2nd 17
   Kido Butai 22, 23, 24, 25, 26, 37, 38, 39, 40, 46, 48, 49, 51, 52, 53, 54, 57, 59, 61, 62, 76; 1st 77, 80, 81–82, 83, 84, 85; 2nd 77
   Koku Sentai: 1st **17**, 17, 20, 21, **22**, 23, 25, 26, 29–30, 46, 47, 52, 58, 77; 2nd **16**, 17, 18, 19, 20, 21, 23, 25, 26, 29–30, 39, 40, 46, 48–49, 52–53, 58, 77, 84–85; 3rd 17; 4th 17, 77; 5th 20, 22, 23, 25, 26, **46**, 46, 47, 48, 53, 54, 57–59, 63, 65
   Kokutai (Ku): 6th 77, 81; 12th 15–16, 20, **2**(41, 92); 13th **7**; 14th 15, 16, 19, 20, **1**(41, 92), **5**(42, 92–93); 31st 53, 54; 32nd 53; 33rd 14, **53**, 53, 54; 35th **53**, 53–54, **95**; 40th 53, 54; Yokosuka 6, 7, **16**, 62
   Mobile Force 63, 64, 69, 70, 71, 74–75
   Naval General Staff 17, 19–20, 22, 24, 76
   Port Moresby Invasion Force 63, 64, 66
   South Seas Force 39, 40, 46, 48, 63
   Southern Force 46, 48

Kakuta, Rear Adm Kakuji 77, 78, 80
Kanno, WO Kenzo 70, 71

Kato, FPO 3/c Motomu 80
Kobayashi, Lt Michio 27, 31, 40, 50, 57, 58, 86, **87**, 87–88, 89
Kondo, Vice Adm Nobutake 46, 48, 49
Koyama, WO Susumu 27, 69
Kuwabara, FPO 2/c Hideyasu 31, 35

Makino, Lt Saburo 34, **36**, 36, 50
McCuskey, Lt(jg) E Scott 87, 88
Midway Atoll 76, 82, **83**, 83; Battle of (1942) 76, 80–91, **87**, **88**, **89**, **90**
Mifuku, Lt Iwakichi 56, 72, 73, 74
Mitsubishi 9; Type 0 Mark 1 Carrier Fighter (A6M2) Zero-sen 15, 25, 38, 39, 40, 46, 47, 50, 56, 64, 77, 79, 82, 86; Type 96 Carrier Fighter (A5M) 8; Type 97 Carrier Attack Aircraft (B5M) 8, 38, 46, 47, 49
Mizuki, FPO 1/c Norinobu 27, 28

Nagahama, FPO 1/c Yoshikazu 49–50
Nagahata, Jun-ichiro 6, 7
Nagumo, Vice-Adm Chuichi 18–19, 22, 25, 37, 38, 39, 49, 52, 55, 57, 59, 81, 82, 83, 84, 85, 86, 91
Nakagawa, WO Shizuo 31, 89
Nakagawa, Lt Takashi 31, 37, 93
Nakajima 9; 6-Shi Carrier-based Special Bomber (D2Y1) 6, 7; 7-Shi Carrier-based Special Bomber (D2N1) 6, 7; 8-Shi Carrier-based Special Bomber 6, 7; 11-Shi Carrier-based Bomber (D3N1) 12, **13**, 13; Type 3 Carrier Fighter (A1N1) 6; Type 90 Mark 2 Reconnaissance Seaplane (E4N3) 7; Type 97 Carrier Attack Aircraft (B5N) 8, 25
Nakajima, WO Yonekichi 36, 37
Nakayama, Ens Shimematsu 31, 89
Nakazawa, WO Iwao 89
Nimitz, Adm Chester W 63, 75

Obuchi, Lt(jg) Keizo 35–36, 37, **8**(43, 94), **56**
Ogawa, Lt Shoichi 34, 50–51, 81, 91
Okada, FPO 3/c Tadao 79
Okamura, FPO 1/c Hidemitsu 87
Ono, Lt Cdr Kanjiro 23, 28
operations: *AL* 76, 77–79; *C* 54, 55–62, **56**, **58**, **60**; *Fu-Go* 19; *MI* 76, 80–91, **87**, **88**, **89**, **90**; *MO* 63, 64–75; *R* **46**, 46–47, **47**, **48**; *S* 18
Oyama, WO Toshio 33
Ozaki, Toshio 9, 10

Pearl Harbour attack (1941) **4**, 23, 24, 25–38, **29**, **30**, **31**, **32**, **33**; Ford Island 23, 24, 25, 28; Haleiwa Field 35; Hickam Field 23, 28; Wheeler Field 23, 24, 27, **28**, 28, 36

Rabaul, New Britain, attacks (1942) **46**, 46–47, **47**
Rogers, 1Lt Robert J 35, 36
Royal Air Force (RAF): No 11 Sqn 61; No 30 Sqn 56; No 258 Sqn 56; No 273 Sqn 61
Royal Navy 54, 57, 61–62; 788 NAS 56; 803 and 806 NASs 61; Eastern Fleet 55, 59; *see also* ships, British

Sakaguchi, FPO 3/c Noburu 34
Sakamoto, Lt Akira 24, **27**, 27, 56, 60, 62
Shimazaki, Lt Cdr Shigekazu 26, 29, 30, 65, 66, 71, 74
Shimizu, FPO 2/c Yoshio 32, **11**(44, 94)
ships, Australian (HMAS): *Gunbar* 50; *Manunda* 51; *Vampire* 60
ships, British (HMS): *Athelstane* (RFA) 61; *Cornwall* 55, **56**, 57–58, **58**, 62; *Dorsetshire* 55, **56**, 57–58, **58**, 62; *Formidable* 55; *Hector* 56; *Hermes* 55, 59–60, **60**, 61, 62; *Hollyhock* 61; *Indomitable* 55, 59; *Lucia* 56; *Tenedos* 56; *Warspite* 55
ships, Dutch 49, 53
ships, Japanese: *Akagi* 16, 17, 20, 23, 37, 46, 48, **49**, 49, **50**, **56**, 58–59, 61, 77, 83, 84, 85, 86, 87, 91; *Chikuma* 52, 83, 86, 87, 89; *Furutaka* 66, 69; *Haruna* 82, 84; *Hiei* 52; *Hiryu* **16**, 16, 17, 24, 37, 40, 48, 49, **50**, 76, 77, 84, 86, **87**, 87, 91; *Hosho* 6,

16, 17; *Junyo* 77, **79**, 79, 80; *Kaga* 16, 17, **26**, **27**, 36, 38, 46, 48, 49, 53, 63, 77, 85, 86, 87, 91; *Kinugasa* 66, 69; *Kirishima* 52; *Mikuma* 91; *Ryujo* 16, 17, **76**, 77; *Shoho* 64, 66, 67, **68**, 68; *Shokaku* **20**, 20, 46, 47, **48**, 54, 57, 63, 64, 69, 74, 75, 77; *Soryu* **16**, 16, 17, 40, 48, 49, 77, 80, 84, 86, 91; *Tone* 52, 57, 58, 61, 82, 83–84, 85; *Zuikaku* 20, **23**, 24, **46**, 46, 47, 48, 54, 57, 63, 64, 69, 74; *see also* Japanese Navy, Imperial: air groups
ships, merchant: *Barossa* 56; *Benledi* 56; *British Motorist* 50, **51**; *British Sergeant* 60; *Don Isidro* 51; *Florence D* 51; *Herstein* 46; *Induna Star* 47; lost at Darwin 50, **51**, 51; *Modjokerto* 52; *Neptuna* 50, **51**; *Norviken* 51; *Van Landsberge* 49; *Westralia* 46; *Zealandia* 51
ships, US (USS): *Admiral Halstead* (USAT) 51; *Arizona* **29**, 33; *California* **29**, 31; *Cassin* **29**, 30, 33; *Dale* 30; *Dobbin* 31; *Downes* **29**, 30; *Edsall* 52; *Enterprise* 24, 29, 39, 48, 54, 64, 80, 81, 84, 85, 86, 91; *Hammann* 91; *Helena* **29**, 31, 32; *Helm* 32; *Honolulu* 31; *Hornet* 64, 80, 81, 84, 85, 91; *Lexington* 24, 63, 65, 66, 68, 69, 70, 71, 72, **73**, 74, **75**, 75; *Maryland* **29**, 32, 33, 34, 36; *Mauna Loa* (USAT) 51; *Meigs* (USAT) 50; *Neosho* 30–31, 32, 64, 65, 66–67, **67**, 75, 84; *Nevada* **32**, 33–34; *New Orleans* 30; *Oklahoma* **29**, 32; *Peary* 50; *Pecos* 52; *Pennsylvania* **29**, 30, 31, 32; *Portmar* 51; *Raleigh* 33; *Saratoga* 39; *Shaw* **31**, 31, 33; *Sims* 65, 66–67, 84; *Tangier* 33; *West Virginia* 31, 34; *William B Preston* 50; *Yorktown* 48, 63, 64, 65, 66, 70, 71, 72–73, **73**, 74, 75, 80, 81, 85–86, **88**, 88–89, **90**, 90, 91
Showa 14
Somerville, Vice Adm Sir James 55, 59
Spruance, Rear Adm Raymond A 80, 81, 82, 83–84
Sugie, FPO 2/c Takeshi 79

Takagi, Vice Adm Takeo 63, 65, 69, 70, 74–75
Takahashi, Lt Cdr Kakuichi **4**, 24, 26, 27, 28, **6**(42, 93), 46, **47**, 56, 59, 60–61, 65, 66, 67, 68, 69, 71, 72, 73
Takahashi, Lt Sadamu 15, 54
Taylor, 2Lt Kenneth M 35, 36
Tomonaga, Lt Joichi 81, **82**, 82, 83, 89, 90
Tsuchiya, FPO 2/c Atsumi **88**, 88

USAAC/USAAF 34–35, 51; 11th FS 78; 18th BW 28; 33rd PS(P) 50, 51; 47th PS 35; 88th Recon. Sqn 37
US Marine Corps: VMF-221 82; VMSB-241 84
US Navy 18, 63; Pacific Fleet 25, 76; Task Force 11 (TF-11) 63–64; TF-14 39, 40; TF-16 64, 80, 81, 83–84, 89; TF-17 64, 65, 66, 68–69, **70**, 70, 71–74, 80, 81, 86; VB-3 85; VB-6 86; VF-2 68, 73; VF-3 85–86, 87; VF-6 89; VF-42 68, 72, 73; VP-14 37; VS-2 71; VS-6 85, 86; VT-3 85, 86; VT-6 85; VT-8 83, 85 *see also* ships, US
Utsuki, FPO 2/c Michiji 35

Watanabe, Lt Toshio 51, 84
Welch, 2Lt George S 35, 36

Yamada, FPO 1/c Kishichiro 32, 88
Yamada, Lt Shohei 32–33, 58
Yamaguchi, Lt Masao 28, 56, 72, 73, 74
Yamaguchi, Rear Adm Tamon 40, 47, 48, 49, 76, 84, 86, 89, 90, 91
Yamakawa, F 1/c Shinsaku 21, 37–38, **9**(43, 94), 52, 77, 79, 80
Yamamoto, Adm Isoroku 17, 18, 19, 22, 54, 62, 63, 75, 76, 80, 91
Yamamoto, Ryozo 6, 7, 12
Yamana, Masao 11
Yamashita, Lt Michiji 30, 31, 51, 60, 87, 88
Yamazaki, FPO 2/c Takeo 34–35, **14**(45, 95), 58
Yokosuka 13-Shi Carrier Bomber (D4Y) 62
Yoshikawa, WO Keijiro 24, 32, 37
Yoshikawa, Takeo 24